T0094031

Medical Ethics
A Reference Guide for Guaranteeing Principled Care and Quality

Medical Ethics
A Reference Guide for Guaranteeing Principled Care and Quality

Eldo E. Frezza, MD, MBA, FACS

Routledge
Taylor & Francis Group

A PRODUCTIVITY PRESS BOOK

A Routledge title, part of the Taylor & Francis imprint, a member of the Taylor & Francis Group, the academic division of T&F Informa plc

Published in 2019 by Routledge
Taylor & Francis Group
711 3rd Avenue
New York, NY 10017

International Standard Book Number-13: 978-1-138-58107-4 (Hardback)

This book contains information obtained from authentic and highly regarded sources. Reprinted material is quoted with permission, and sources are indicated. A wide variety of references are listed. Reasonable efforts have been made to publish reliable data and information, but the author and the publisher cannot assume responsibility for the validity of all materials or for the consequences of their use.

Library of Congress Cataloging-in-Publication Data

Names: Frezza, Eldo E., author.
Title: Medical ethics : a reference guide for guaranteeing principled care and quality / Eldo Frezza.
Description: Boca Raton : Taylor & Francis, 2019. | Includes bibliographical references and index.
Identifiers: LCCN 2018020483 (print) | LCCN 2018022124 (ebook) | ISBN 9780429506949 (e-Book) | ISBN 9781138581074 (hardback : alk. paper)
Subjects: | MESH: Ethics, Medical
Classification: LCC R724 (ebook) | LCC R724 (print) | NLM W 50 | DDC 174.2--dc23
LC record available at https://lccn.loc.gov/2018020483

Visit the Taylor & Francis Web site at
http://www.taylorandfrancis.com

This book is in memory of Dr Sherilyn Gordon-Burroughs
and to all women who were victims of domestic violence.

We trained in the same university. She called me one day and told me
to write a book on medical ethics. She encouraged me to
start the project and left all of us all too early.

Contents

SECTION IV   RESOURCES ALLOCATIONS

SECTION V   PHYSICIAN WELLNESS AND MORAL DISTRESS

SECTION VI QUALITY AND DIGNITY

Preface

This is not intended to be another ethics book. It is a guide and handbook, which physicians, residents, students, and health care providers can carry and use as a quick reference. This book is intended to look at the ethics problems we faced every day, give the background to the ethics problem, and give practical advice that can be quickly reviewed during a busy day. It is not a textbook but a guidebook.

A vital strength of this book is that it has a multidisciplinary approach from professions such as health care practitioners (doctors, nurses, surgeons, midwives, etc.), alongside lawyers, social scientists, civil servants, and theologians.

In this book, we start with an introduction of the ethics subjects. We then discuss how ethics should be for everyone and then approach the most burning issues the health care provider faces in the daily practice.

Ethical teaching should be an active part of the medical students' and administrators' training. Ethics should be taught in four divisions: basic ethics, clinical ethics, legal principles relating to ethics, and the ethics of research and affiliation. The book addresses the need to understand who has the right to health care, the justice of clinical practice, what autonomy means for a patient giving consent, who is going to make any surrogate decision, and so on.

We hope that this way this nebulous idea of ethics will then turn into a more practical vision and be useful for all people who want to practice medicine. To help the process, we summarize the concepts of each chapter in a simple table at the end, "The Ethics Table."

Other Publications

Tony Hope. *Medical Ethics A Very Short Introduction*: 1st edition: Oxford University Press, 2004.

Jonathan Herring. *Medical Law and Ethics*: 4th edition: Oxford University Press, 2012.

Hope, R. A., Savulescu J., and Hendrick J. *Medical Ethics and Law – The Core Curriculum*: Churchill, Livingstone, 2003.

L. Schwartz, P. E. Preece, and R. A. Hendry. *Medical Ethics: A Case-Based Approach*: Edinburgh, WB Saunders, 2003.

C. Baxter, M. Brennan, Y. Coldicott, and M. Moller. *Medical Ethics & Law*: 2nd edition: PasTest, 2005.

H. Kuhse and P. Singer (eds.). *Bioethics an Anthology*: Blackwell, 2001.

P. Benn. *Ethics*: Routledge, 2002.

R. Gillon. *Philosophical Medical Ethics*: John Wiley, 1985.

J. Harris. *The Value of Life*: Routledge,1991.

J. Jackson. *Ethics in Medicine*: Polity Press, 2006.

B. Jennet. *The Vegetative State*: Cambridge University Press, 2002.

Author

 **Eldo E. Frezza** was born and raised in Venice, attended Medical School in Italy, and completed his postgraduate course as a resident in the United States. He also obtained a Masters in Business Administration from Texas Tech University. He is a Fellow of the American College of Surgeons (FACS), American Medical Association, and American Medical Physician Leadership.

Dr. Frezza is an award-winning physician executive who elevates organizational performance and aligns physicians to rapidly changing health care landscapes. He embraces and skillfully navigates the challenges of complex enterprises including, rural hospitals, academic medical centers, and physician practices. His clinical background as a surgeon informs his ability to thrive in a high-pressure environment, assess complex business situations, and perform thoughtful analysis to identify affordable, sustainable solutions.

CEO and founder of Cure Your Practice (www.cureyourpractice.com), Dr. Frezza has over 20 years of experience providing consulting services to health care organizations in the areas of metrics, supply chains, clinical service line development, organizational strategy, alignment, and network formation. This includes health care systems, academic medical centers, physician groups, insurance companies and government agencies, as well as professional organizations.

As a medical director of quality and vice president of medical affairs, he has guided the boardroom decision making that has defined the priorities and direction of many leading health care organizations to keep high quality and ethics values.

Dr. Frezza is the author of three essential textbooks on ethics, business, and laparoscopic surgery and numerous articles on clinical practice, research, economics, and ethics. He is also the author of several books on sociology and fiction. Dr. Frezza has written eight books with well-known publishers and has published more than 200 articles in peer review journals and book chapters. His bestselling book is a diet book, which continues to sell ten years after his second edition.

Dr. Frezza has written books for his college classes and tested them on his students. He is always working on motivation and how to make society better by teaching, demonstrating, and explaining the basic principles of societal ethics, civic responsibility, and wellness. These opportunities have helped students find a better pathway in life. Dr. Frezza makes his books easy to read, to which his students attest that the attraction of his writing is that the book can be read in a single sitting.

He has been a full professor and professor of ethics in several institutions, among them Texas A&M, Texas Tech, University of Pittsburgh, and the like. He has won several writing contests, is a regular speaker on ethics, sociology, and medicine for different medical societies, and is an editor of medical journals.

Dr. Frezza started as a journalist before going to medical school. He speaks three languages; he has often been considered a Renaissance man since his background goes across medical specialties into ethics, business, sociology, and philosophy.

He also served as commander of the Texas Medical Ranger for West Texas.

PUBLIC HEALTH

I

Chapter 1

Medical Ethics from Hippocrates to the AMA

Ethics is a significant part of life for anybody and health care providers especially. Ethics is the study of moral character and is consistent in the belief that the practice of medicine is based on perfect character and behavior toward another person.

What are our sources of ethics in life? Family, religion, life experience, historical perspective, personal training, education, profession, etc.

Medical ethics define the duty of the physician toward the patient. The Hippocratic Oath is its foundation. But before Hippocrates, even in our earliest history, we find evidence of ethics in treating patients by either the priests that were taking care of the patients or by the lay people who were selected as physicians.[1]

The Art of Medicine

Hippocrates was the first to initiate the idea of ethics being applied to those who were treating patients. Initially, the concept was quite simple, for example, having a physician to provide uncompensated care, not to assistant with suicide or abortion, and so forth. These ideas evolved in a more sophisticated direction and were debated and updated at different times throughout history.

Hippocrates believed the art of medicine is threefold: (1) to relieve pain, (2) to reduce the violence of disease, and (3) to refrain from trying to cure those whom the disease has conquered, acknowledging that in such cases medicine is powerless.

He also believed that if there is an opportunity to serve a stranger in financial straits, one should give full assistance, for the love of humankind and the love of medical art go together.

The most well-known passage from the writings of Hippocrates is the following: "premium, non nocere," translated from Latin to English as "to help or at least to do no harm." His concept of not doing harm could have meant doing nothing at that time, and that was acceptable. This was probably the first concept of ethics ever described in medical and human history.

Hippocrates set forth some essential precepts. These principles remain the principles applied to our medical profession today.

History of Ethics

The history of ethics in medicine goes back to Christian, Islamic, and Jewish scholarship and theology. But it wasn't until the 19th century that medical ethics even had a name.

In 1803, Sir Thomas Percival[2] published a thesis entitled, "A Code of Institutes and Precepts Adapted to the Professional Conduct of Physicians and Surgeons." According to Percival, physicians should "unite tenderness with steadiness and condescension with authority, as to inspire the minds of their patients with gratitude, respect, and confidence." The book was created from his passion for jurisprudence.

In 1847 at the American Medical Association's first meeting, they adopted the first American code of medical ethics. It was based on Dr. Percival's work. The code remained mostly unchanged until 1957 when a distinction between medical etiquette and medical ethics was deemed necessary.

Joseph Fletcher, the founder of the theory of situational ethics, wrote *Morals and Medicine* in 1954, establishing himself as the father of bioethics. His premise of reasoned choice empowered more significant technological advancement in medicine and higher patient education as well.

Ethics and Deontology

Ethics is a study of morality and defining what is right or wrong. One's first experience with ethics comes from one's family, religion, background, historical perspective, personal training, and education. The line of conduct was initially illustrated by Freud combining self-defacement, self-sacrifice, compassion, and the intensity of our actions. The following issues are illustrated by Freud:

- Self-defacement
- Self-sacrifice
- Compassion
- Integrity

Deontology is the way people judge the morality and the actions of others based on rules. Rules come initially from family education, but they are more defined by philosophers. Jeremy Bentham in his book in 1926 described the "five types of ethical theory." In it, we find the concept that there is a duty and obligation to obey the code of conduct, and every action has a consequence from which the word "consequentialism" derived. So, if morality and duty exist, a consequentialist judgment of those actions is always behind it.

Immanuel Kant expressed the concept of morality as the right thing is to do one's duty by each person. Morality is based on the actions of a person and not on their motive. He was advocating the highest good for everybody. When it is suitable only for oneself, it is not always a good action. Intelligence, pleasure, and perseverance aren't just good but sometimes are good by itself, and they don't meet the qualification to be good for everybody. Happiness is good for the person that provided the comfort. Therefore, it is not a quality that can be enjoyed by all people. Thus, the only good that is applicable to everyone is the goodwill that we, as people, can be of use to everyone.

Kant was suggesting that we can do good inside or outside of the law and wrong within the law without being good. Therefore, what should be pushing us toward action is the motive of goodwill, not because of authority or duty. This is an exciting concept when applied in the business world, and we will discuss this later in this chapter.

To summarize Kant's vision: (1) you need to act toward a universal good, (2) you need to treat others as you treat your family, with a simple and positive mean, and (3) you need to act like it would be the best thing for humanity. Therefore, there is not an absolute right or an absolute wrong, but there are evil or good intentions and these have consequences. Even a lie could be useful if the motive is goodwill.

Deontology did not come from religion or follow God's commandments. Only later did some faiths influence deontology. In 2006, Frances Kamm published a book in which he described new theories. He said that harming a person is terrible but can be good if it is done to save others. This was intended to explain the moral differences between the consequences and other consequences of the action and the constraint of observance of the law. Iain King, in his book *How to Make Good Decisions and be Right All the Time* (2008), modifies some of the deontological principles, which are compatible with ethics and consequences. Therefore, he judges the morality of the action according to the implications of the action, which is different from the earlier theory.

A proper learning experience can influence and encourage students to explore and develop their moral ethics. They can develop their boundaries, and most importantly, they will not be afraid to say "no" because they know where to draw the line; they know better.[3]

This can be compared to the famous old saying "give a man a fish; he eats for a day. Teach a man to fish, and he eats for a lifetime."

If we apply this idea, we can make the next generation an epitome of managerial leadership, which can eventually teach the next generation how to "fish," making the business world safer! They need to understand their personal experiences and their community to build their subjective morality, and then they need to have role models on which they can base their objective morality. With this foundation, they will know how to act in the "real world."

Societal Values

We need to return to human and societal values. Most of the time, respect for human life, honesty, and fairness are chosen. After you write down the essential values, see if you carry them out, your subjective action of morality, and then see if those values apply to your business. If you can make objective choices, then see if your employees can. If you discover flaws in this process, then you have a problem, and perhaps your customers have identified the problem before you and that is why you are losing them.

Principle or moral courage is significant because when you have a conflict of ethics with another person, only your courage can bring you to discuss it despite the pressure imposed by corporate structure, authority, and politics. Saying "no" could pose a risk. At times "evil" can be stronger than our principles.

Only in literature is the human embodiment of evil given an identity. Thus, Iago in Shakespeare's *Othello* proclaims with pride:

> Divinity of Hell! When devils will the blackest sins put on, they do suggest at first with heavenly shows, as I do now … I'll pour this pestilence into his ear.[4]

In 19th century opera, villains are given arias to sing. Thus, Verdi's *Otello* has Iago stating:

> I believe in a cruel god, who has created me in his image and whom, in hate, I name.

In real life, however, evil people don't publicly state that they are evil.

The Search for Guidelines

Can we rely on guidelines to help us meet the self-challenge of determining our principles for behaving honorably in our professional lives and ethically in general? Do to others what you would like to be done to you is an impeccable guideline. This guideline is the first principle of self-determination to start our professional lives.

Why, as physicians, should we not turn to the Oath of Hippocrates, the essence of which has been summarized by many in the admonition – "Primum, non nocere," or "First, not harm"? Primarily because that precept is not found in the Oath of Hippocrates. It may well be a Latin translation of Hippocrates but from his *Epidemics*,[5] BK.I, Section XI, wherein Hippocrates states:

> Declare the past, diagnose the present, foretell the future; practice these acts. As to diseases, make a habit of two things – to help, or at least to not harm.

More to the point, we harm to do good. By doing surgery, we harm the person on whom we are doing surgery in order to obtain a good outcome.

The Professional Code of Ethics

In 1847, these words were mostly repeated in the first Code of Medical Ethics[6] of the American Medical Association (AMA), adopted at the first AMA Convention in Philadelphia of 268 physicians from 22 states.

The AMA has written nine principles.

- Respect human life
- Refrain from supporting committing crimes
- Treat the sick and injury with competence
- Retain knowledge and skill
- Protect privacy and confidentiality
- Work freely with colleagues
- Develop and promote advancing medicine
- Advise the public about present and future medicine
- Teach and mentor those who follow these principles

The AMA Code of Ethics

The AMA Code of Medical Ethics has undergone multiple revisions. In 1958,[7] the Code was reduced to ten principles of medical ethics; in 1980,[8] to seven principles; and to nine principles in 2001.[9] The work of the AMA was supplemented in 1973 by the Patient's Bill of Rights published by the American Hospital Association, which emphasizes full disclosure of diagnoses, prognoses, treatment options, and the patient's right to refuse treatment.

Outside the United States, the World Medical Association (WMA) has published eight separate declarations of ethics, including the Declaration of Geneva and the International Code of Medical Ethics in 1948 and the Declaration of Helsinki in 1964. The latter focused on the principle of informed consent for volunteers in biomedical research and was an outgrowth of the Nuremberg Code issued after the trial of Nazi doctors who had experimented with Jewish prisoners in concentration camps in World War II.

The AMA Code of Medical Ethics, similar codes, and the various medical oaths that have been promulgated over time, all have in common a social contract not only between physicians but among physicians, patients, and society. By the 1847 AMA Code, the AMA set licensing requirements and minimal education standards and promised to drive out the unscrupulous from the ranks of medical practitioners. In the 1958 Principles of Medical Ethics, Section 10 reads:

> The honored ideals of the medical profession imply that the responsibilities of the physician extend not only to the individual but also to a society where these responsibilities deserve his interest and participation in activities which have the purpose of improving both the health and the well-being of the individual and the community.

In the 1980 Principles, Principle VII states that

> A physician shall recognize a responsibility to participate in activities contributing to an improved community.

The Principles of 2001 reiterate the above and adds a Principle IX:

> A physician shall support access to medical care for all people.

The AMA has responded to present day concerns that have arisen for physicians with its principle of medical ethics. They are not laws but standards of conduct by which we define as essential to honorable behavior by physicians.

1. A physician shall be dedicated to providing competent medical care with compassion and respect for human dignity and rights.
2. A physician shall uphold the standards of professionalism, be honest in all professional interactions, and strive to report physicians with incompetences or engaged in fraud or deception to appropriate entities (from Chapter 10: Physician Ethical And Legal Issues Flashcards).
3. A physician shall respect the law and also recognize a responsibility to seek changes to those requirements that are contrary to the best interests of the patient.
4. A physician shall respect the rights of patients, colleagues, and other health professionals and shall safeguard patient confidences and privacy within the constraints of the law.
5. A physician shall continue to study, apply, and advance scientific knowledge, maintain a commitment to medical education, make relevant information available to patients, colleagues, and the public, obtain consultation, and use the talents of other health professionals when required.

6. A physician shall, in the provision of appropriate patient care, except in emergencies, be free to choose whom to serve, with whom to associate, and the environment in which to provide medical care.
7. A physician shall recognize a responsibility to participate in activities contributing to the improvement of the community and the betterment of public health.
8. A physician shall, while caring for a patient, regard responsibility to the patient as paramount.
9. A physician shall support access to medical care for all people.

Notes

1. Frezza, E. 2018. Ethics necessary in health care: A review. *Biometrics & Biostatics Int J.* Accessed at URL: http://medcraveonline.com/BBIJ/BBIJ-07-00224.p
2. Leake C. D., ed. 1927. *Percival's Medical Ethics.* Baltimore, MD: Williams & Wilkins; pp. 1–291.
3. Frezza, E. 2017. Ethics and deontology in business. *Austin J of Business Admin and Management,* 1(2). Accessed at URL: http://austinpublishinggroup.com/business-administration-and-management/download.php?file=fulltext/ajbam-v1-id1007.pdf
4. Shakespeare, W. *Othello, Act II, Scene III, Lines 356-359; 362, Shakespeare the Complete Works,* (ed,. Harrison G. B.). New York, NY: Harcourt Brace and Company.
5. Hippocrates. *Epidemics, Book I, Section XI,* (Tr. By Jones W.H.S., (ed. M.B. Strauss)). In *Familiar Medical Quotations,* (ed. Strauss M.B.). London, UK: J. & A. Churchill, Ltd. 625.
6. Code of Medical Ethics of the American Medical Association, Original 1847 Version. Accessed at URL: http://www.ama-assn.org/ama/pub/category/4256.html
7. American Medical Association Principles of Medical Ethics, 1958 Version. Accessed at URL: http://www.ama-assn.org/ama/pub/category/4256.html
8. American Medical Association Principles of Medical Ethics, 1980 Version. Accessed at URL: http://www.ama-assn.org/ama/pub/category/4256.html
9. American Medical Association Principles of Medical Ethics, 2001 Revised Version. Accessed at URL: http://www.ama-assn.org/ama/pub/category/4256.html

Suggested Reading

1. Beauchamp, T. L. 1991. *Philosophical Ethics: An Introduction to Moral Philosophy,* 2nd edn. New York, NY: McGraw Hill.
2. Broad, C. D. 1930. *Five Types of Ethical Theory.* New York, NY: Harcourt Brace and Co.
3. Flew, A. 1979. Consequentialism. In *A Dictionary of Philosophy,* 2nd edn. New York, NY: St Martins.
4. Kant, I. 1964. *Groundwork of the Metaphysic of Morals.* New York, NY. HarperCollins.
5. Kamm, F. M. 2006. *Intricate Ethics Rights, Responsibilities, and Permissible Harm Rights, Responsibilities, and Permissible Harm.* New York, NY: Oxford University Press.

6. King, I. 2008. *How to Make Good Decisions and be Right all the Time.* London, UK: Bloomsbury Publishing.
7. Olson, R. G. 1967. Deontological ethics. In P. Edwards (ed.) *The Encyclopedia of Philosophy.* London, UK: Collier Macmillan.
8. Ross, W. D. 1930. *The Right and the Good.* Oxford, UK: Clarendon Press.
9. Salzman, T. A. 1995. *Deontology and Teleology: An Investigation of the Normative Debate in Roman Catholic Moral Theology.* Leuven, Belgium: Leuven University Press.
10. Waller, B. N. 2005. *Consider Ethics: Theory, Readings, and Contemporary Issues.* New York, NY: Pearson Longman.

Ethics Summary Table

Ethics and You, The Physician

The physician needs to learn the art of medicine which are:

Relieve pain
Reduce diseases
Understand family situation
Respect end of life
Show integrity in their actions
Retain knowledge and skill
Work professionally and freely
Support medical access for people
Recognize the limitations of practice
Recognize the boundary of the law
Apply their best judgment

Chapter 2

Changes in Health Care and the Physician's Role

The health care industry, nonexistent a century ago, is now a considerable fraction of the U.S. economy and a tricky business with a multitude of legislative problems. Understanding how this behemoth arose from dealing with such issues as no insurance, to pay per case and, lastly, to capitation, requires a historical context. This chapter reviews the recent history of the health care industry, dividing it into six parts, evaluates how hospitals today make and lose money, and provides a few projections about the future of health care in the United States.

First Insurance

It has been an adventure to evaluate the health care evolution; the health care industry was nonexistent one century ago.

In 1930, Justin Kimbal created the first U.S. health care insurance, the Blue Cross, under the border of trust of the University of Texas.

Cost Reimbursement

Most hospitals were nonprofit corporations. When people could pay, they were given a bill and the payment method chosen was cost reimbursement.

First Health Maintenance Organization (HMO) and Capitation Payment

In the effort to recruit workers for producing ships during the war in 1940, Kaiser Shipbuilding Company offered employee health benefits to facilitate recruitment. By implementing this insurance, Kaiser ensured insurance and benefits only to the employees who participated in the deal. This was, in perspective, the first HMO. The payment was set from the start of employment. This payment or capitation was obstructed by medical society. Many physicians did not ask to participate.

No HMO Restrictions

In 1980, federal legislation abolished all such restrictions, and HMOs began to spread across the country. Many existing insurances adopted the capitation system to control cost and make profits.

Eight Stages of Health Care Revolution

Stage 1

Care was determined by the availability of the hospital, and it was organized on a fee-for-service basis.

Stage 2

In 1970, it was pay-for-service in hospitals. Because of this, hospitals were making lots of money and more hospitals were built.

Stage 3

The 1980s gave birth to prospective payment through insurance.
 The most crucial innovation at this time was fixed-pricing.
 The diagnosis-related group or DRG six payments to a specific diagnosis.
 Payment for a particular diagnosis changed the average hospital stay from 13 to 7 days.

Stage 4

In the late 1980s, downsizing eliminated unprofitable programs and duplicate facility hospitals worked hard to consolidate themselves into the corporation chain, which at that point was a difficult transition.

HMO was reborn in 1990 as a revenue source for the hospital.

Physicians were given a fixed amount per patient per month to provide specific services; therefore, physicians concentrated on illness prevention.

Stage 5

In the late 1990s, there was concern about the quality of health care.

Under capitation, the need to avoid unnecessary hospital admissions decreased the length of the patient's stay and resulted in the prevention of illness.

It was necessary for physicians to maintain comprehensive medical records.

The starting bonus for a physician was based on the number of days that the physician keeps the patient in the hospital to charge to the cost plans.

There was an increase in the patient paying out-of-pocket.

Stage 6

The new development is that many hospitals have been incorporated into a corporation that consists of hundreds of hospitals, therefore, most of the administrative positions have been cut and a lot of purchasing and decisions are now done at a central location. Consequently, many jobs have been cut in the name of health care cost margins, the power of HMOs has been increasing, and physicians have been losing power. Now, hospitals face the same problem that the physicians faced years ago, because the HMO is dictating the care.

Stage 7

The Affordable Care Act (ACA) legislation passed in 2010 included the following points:

- Increased access to care – Medicaid expansion, insurance mandate
- Improved quality of care – fee-for-service vs. value-based purchasing
- Reduced health care costs
- Population health
- Coordinated care through health care delivery systems

Stage 8

Unsecure access to care – Medicaid reduction since the new health care law passed late 2017 included the following points:

- Improved quality of care – value-based purchasing
- Reduced health care costs
- Coordinated care through health care delivery systems

How to Keep Up with the Changing Faces of Health Care

The nature of public health is changing today. This is due to:

Low reimbursement
Inflation of insurances
Multiple health care providers involved in the care
Increase in government oversight
Invasion of managed care regulation
Greater liability risk

The physician's role as a position of authority or captain of the ship has been lost in the culture shift and now the role is much more focused as being part of a team formed by medical and nonmedical personnel. This shift has increased physician frustration due to a perceived loss of autonomy.

A movement from the medical society has begun to create a culture of professionalism and safety.

With regard to patient safety, behavior that interferes with the ability of others to carry out their duties and that efficiently undermines the patient's confidence in the hospital has been eliminated.

In a study in 2003, safe medication practices showed that 49% of health care providers, nurses, and pharmacists had problems with order clarification due to experiences of intimidation from a physician.

The doctor's ultimate goal is to be committed to patient care and to clarity.

Self-Determination

For self-determination to guide us in achieving professionalism and ethics in medicine, we must have personal autonomy. We are taught by the variety of human nature. We acknowledge our fallibility and our power to harm. Ours is a profession where decisions are singular and the responsibility is heavy. Thus, when a physician reaches professional maturity, that individual has achieved personal autonomy.

On the broad scope of freedom, we are allowed only a small arc, and that arc is narrowed daily by the administrative policies of academia, hospitals, insurance companies, and government. We are being reduced to "vendors" of health care; this status is not a firm base for the autonomy necessary for self-determination in our profession.

The Individual and the Group

Today most decisions are made by a group – an elected legislative body, an appointed judicial body, or an ad hoc team of consultants. This is true in government, in industry, in universities, and indeed in health care. There is comfort in the rule of the majority. In all these affairs of governance there is a head, a president, and a chief executive officer, and the achievements, as well as the place in the history of these organizations, are identified with that leader, for good and for ill.

The "Talmud" poses four self-challenges expressed as four questions of self-determination:

1. Have I lived honorably on a daily basis?
2. Have I raised the next generation?
3. Have I set aside time for study?
4. Have I lived hopefully?

Safety

Physicians are expected to establish and enforce the standard on safety, self-regulation, and professional responsibility. The physician is expected to develop and implement the rules.

Health care organizations emphasize the focus on customer service.

Collaboration is reviewing each other's performance and having input into team decisions, regardless of power in rank strategy.

Promoting professional behavior and patient safety is an essential step in establishing a fundamental change to health care culture, including the possibility to disclose adverse events such as medical errors.

Collection of professional behavior continues to grow more evident, and more appropriate strategies should be applied.

The *clinical mistakes* of others limited modernistic learning from personal error, and this is a part of our learning process. The use of discussion and the use of the morbidity and mortality meeting are focused toward an increase in sensibility and increase skill.

The Attitude of Physicians Toward Their Profession

What does it mean to practice medicine? Much has been written in medical education literature and has been informed, to some extent, by accrediting regulatory and standard-setting agencies that seek to define what it means to be a physician. More recently, these efforts translate into lengthy descriptions or checklists that focus on an extensive body of knowledge and skill sets required of physicians. The need to understand and reflect upon the personal attributes and professional responsibilities, which are intrinsic to being a physician, particularly when navigating into a career in the profession of medicine, is essential. This alignment helps to clarify and reinforce the meaning of a physician throughout one's professional growth and development.

A physician must:

- Be caring
- Be inquisitive
- Be civic minded

Suggested Reading

1. American College of Surgeons. Fellowship Pledge. Accessed at URL: http://www.facs.org/fellows_info/statements/stonprin.html#fp.
2. American Hospital Association. 1978. A patient's bill of rights. In W. T. Reich (ed.) *The Encyclopedia of Bioethics*. New York, NY: The Free Press; 1978.
3. American Medical Association Principles of Medical Ethics, 1958 Version. Accessed at URL: http://www.ama-assn.org/ama/pub/category/4256.html.
4. American Medical Association Principles of Medical Ethics, 1980 Version. Accessed at URL: http://www.ama-assn.org/ama/pub/category/4256.html.
5. American Medical Association Principles of Medical Ethics, 2001 Revised Version. Accessed at URL: http://www.ama-assn.org/ama/pub/category/4256.html.
6. Code of Medical Ethics of the American Medical Association, Original 1847 Version. Accessed at URL: http://www.ama-assn.org/ama/pub/category/4256.html.
7. The Babylonian Talmud. Tractate Shabbat; 31a. Accessed at URL: https://www.sefaria.org/texts/Talmud.

Ethics Summary Table

How to Be Professional

A physician should:

Maintain professional competence throughout one's career.
Deal honestly with patients.
Respect patient confidentiality.
Avoid inappropriate relations with patients.
Improve his scientific knowledge.
Fulfill professional responsibilities.
Improve the quality of health care.
Advocate improved and equitable access to care.
Support the just distribution of limited resources.
Maintain trust by managing conflicts of interest.

Chapter 3

Ethical Issues in Health Care and Medical School Curricula

Not Only in Medical School

Medical schools have introduced ethics into their curricula. But curricula needs to be included in the health care system, hospitals, and health care corporations. They need to all work together.

The essential requirement for the future success of the health care system is reported in Table 3.1. This will help empower students, tomorrow's professionals, to make better decisions regarding their role in medicine. The same should be valid for those working in an administrative position. Medicine must have a culture of safety instilled in all workers before they enter the hospital care system. Only through a consistent ethical code and strict deontology taught alongside anatomy as a necessary requirement to work in medicine can we create this culture of safety.

We must provide new personnel working in health care with a conceptual tool to navigate through the ethical issues that they will encounter in clinical practice. Necessary steps need to be taken during their training that focus on discussion, example, and fundamental principles.

Ethics should be taught at four levels: basic ethics, clinical ethics, legal laws relating to ethics, and the ethics of research and affiliation. Health care professionals need to understand who has the right to health care, the justice of clinical practice, what autonomy means for a patient giving consent, who is going to make any surrogate decision, and so on. Case-based examples are one of the best tools to help them in this study.

Table 3.1   Ethics in Health Care

Mandatory curricula in medical school
Consistent code of ethics
Foundational culture of safety
Health care justice
Clinical ethics
Legal principles
Health professional curricula
Hospital CEO curricula
System curricula
Health care corporation curricula
Health resources
Ethics framework for hospital
Patient's need first

The culture of safety will not be healthy if ethics studies stop after the first or second year of medical school. Ethics studies should continue into the third and fourth year rotation and into daily practice. This can be applied to hospitals, health professionals, and health care systems as they follow through with their physicians to ensure that those principles are applied.

We then not only welcome more teaching of ethics within a more standardized framework but these students will be the professionals who will develop a consistent code of ethical principles and will be the hospital administrators, applying these same standards.

The new culture of safety they will create and maintain will benefit doctors, health care workers, at every level, and most of all, patients.

We can divide the teaching of ethics into different sections. Among those are value, autonomy, beneficence, nonmaleficence, respect of human rights, euthanasia, informed consent, confidentiality, importance of communication, control, and resolution. Ethics committees set guidelines for each of these.

A foundational tenet of ethics in medical practice, as in many professions, is a conflict of interest. Transparency is of utmost importance where physicians' relationships are concerned. The futility of medical care and the futility of information are also significant concerns in bioethics.

These values are based on a respect for autonomy. A patient has a right to refuse treatment. They must be able to trust the beneficence of the physician; that the doctor is working in their best interest. Justice is another factor. Health resources must be available in a way that any patient who needs them can access them. This last has the United States on the horns of a dilemma, like all medical care.

Ethics at All Levels of Health Care

The tradition of deontology and ethics theory is based on virtues as defined in consequentialism, with the goal of doing no harm and supporting the good for all. This should be the foundational value of every medical career. This is the ideal rule for a physician because they are professionals that always need to consider the benefit of all as surely as they are careful not to harm the patient.

When difficulties arise, the physician should look back at their values and ethics to formulate the solution. We suggest, therefore, that any doctor or medical students should have an "ethical framework" on which they base their practice and on which they base their line of conduct.

This same framework is equally applicable to the chief executive officer (CEO), chief medical officer (CMO), chief financial officer (CFO), and directors of the hospital. It is vital that the whole hospital and the health care system subscribe to the same code.

Two essential parts accompany this ethical framework – the subjective and objective. The individual is about dealing with the patient. To be effective here, you need to understand their background and culture to better apply your clinical judgment and offer solutions.

The subjective must be evaluated and it must be understood how they will frame your practice and your clinical judgment. It is an integral part of a hospital and health care system to mount their "business" in a way that the whole organization can follow certain principles.

The objective must be agreed to by each participant and an understanding reached about how ethics will apply to your practice.

It is essential for a hospital and health care system to frame its business in a way that the whole organization can follow certain principles. The patient is the physician's customer, and the physician is the system's customer. Therefore, a consistent ethical code needs to be applied by the health system toward the physician and by the physician toward the patient. This helps ensure a constant discernment for greater mutual understanding and organization.

How to Solve Ethical Issues

How do we solve ethical issues? By clarification of the value of the physician and the benefits. This is true for everybody from physicians to students, from administrators to nurses. Most of the time, an ethical meeting and committee will help in framing some of these issues, but the reality is that this type of committee works on demand, and therefore, only when problems arise does this comes into play. To be a successful hospital or successful health organization, the ethical frame should have been put in place when the hospital opened, or the health care system was developed. For a physician or administrator of the hospital, we should stop and write the ten most important values which will guide our practice or guide our hospital in the ideal society. The constraints are imposed by daily practice, by the corporate structure, by the hospital, by politics, and by authority, which limits our ability to address issues. An excellent medical school, a good hospital, or a good health organization should represent the location where we can find the answer and should not be the means of constriction.

Medical School Curricula

In medical schools, it is important to have physicians as role models. However, in health care systems, it is necessary to have administrators as role models. Both must focus on discussions which involve professional development, responsibilities, legal and ethical principles, research, and deontology. Therefore, both should go for training and have a curriculum in ethics.

We suggest ethics and bioethical curricula as laid out in Table 3.2 and extracurricular study based on clinical experiences and problem-oriented samples as laid out in Table 3.3.

Residency Program

Even in a residency program, the code of ethics is introduced, and residency programs periodically grade the residents on these principles of professionalism, which are summarized as

- Demonstrate respect, compassion, and integrity
- Responsiveness to the needs of patients that supersedes self-interest
- Commitment to excellence and ongoing professional development
- Demonstrate a commitment to ethical principles regarding patient confidentiality, informed consent, and business practice
- Demonstrate sensitivity

The Future

We realize that it is complicated to implement consistent ethical principles in health care and that is why we need to start with medical students and future

Table 3.2 Ethical and Bioethical Curriculum

Ethics
Professionalism and responsibilities
Codes of ethics
Confidentiality (where and with whom to talk)
Informed consent: Commitment to honesty
Autonomy and limitations
Conflict of interest
Non-compliant patients
Sexual harassment
Medical records
Telemedicine
Bioethics
Justice in clinical practice and legal, regulatory environments
The right to health care
Transplant organs
Autonomy
Decision making
Refusal of treatment and justified paternalism
Advance directives and proxies
Ethical dangers of human subject research
The importance of research and the development of new therapies
The common rule: Requirements for the ethical conduct of research

hospital administrators. To a high degree, health care has become a business and patients have had much of their autonomy stolen in this business culture. But the customers (the patients) will eventually understand who is conducting themselves with consistent ethics and will remain loyal to that physician/hospital.

Only by setting up new physicians and new health systems that are ethical, will health care have a stable, solid foundation upon which to grow. Fraud, mistreating employees, and mismanaging finances will quickly bring any business down like a house of cards.

Table 3.3 Extra Curricula for Students While on the Job (Residency or Starting in Hospitals)

Small group discussion
Case-based ethics issues
Participating in ethics committees
End-of-life service rotation
Clinical skill practice
Deontology and ethics reasoning
Burnout
Health insurance
Abusive patients

Investing in students and residents and new hiring is also significant. It ensures our future.

Chapter from the Article

Frezza, E. E. & Frezza, G. E. 2017. Ethics is necessary for the medical student to health administrator. *Journal of Epidemiology and Infectious Disease* 1(1): 2–6.

Suggested Reading

1. Beauchamp, T. L. 1991. *Philosophical Ethics: An Introduction to Moral Philosophy*, 2nd edn. New York, NY: McGraw Hill.
2. Broad, C. D. 1930. *Five Types of Ethical Theory*. New York, NY: Harcourt Brace and Co.
3. Flew, A. 1979. Consequentialism. In *A Dictionary of Philosophy*, 2nd edn. New York, NY: St Martins.
4. Flew, Antony. 1979. Consequentialism. In *A Dictionary of Philosophy* (2nd Ed.). New York, NY: St Martins.
5. Kant, I. 1964. *Groundwork of the Metaphysics of Morals*. New York, NY: Harper and Row Publishers, Inc.
6. Kamm, F. M. Professor of Philosophy Harvard University (2006). *Intricate Ethics Rights, Responsibilities, and Permissible Harm Rights, Responsibilities, and Permissible Harm*. Oxford University Press.
7. King, I. 2008. *How to Make Good Decisions and Be Right All the Time*. London: Bloomsbury Publishing.
8. Olson, R. G. 1967. Deontological ethics. In P. Edwards (ed.) *The Encyclopedia of Philosophy*. London: Collier Macmillan.

9. Ross, W. D. 1930. *The Right and the Good.* Oxford: Clarendon Press.
10. Salzman, T. A. 1995. *Deontology and Teleology: An Investigation of the Normative Debate in Roman Catholic Moral Theology.* Leuven, Belgium: Leuven University Press.
11. Waller, B. N. 2005. *Consider Ethics: Theory, Readings, and Contemporary Issues.* New York, NY: Pearson Longman.

Ethics Summary Table

How to Teach Ethics and Where

Ethics is the base for health professionals.

Doctors and administration should have the same ethics background.

Medical school needs to introduce more clear curricula.

Administrators in hospitals should attend ethics courses.

Ethics is the right ending of our soul.

The good end should drive the decision when in doubt.

An ethics committee is a must nowadays.

Chapter 4

Public Health and Professionalism

Health Delivery

The changes in the health care delivery system and the nature of the medical profession has tempted physicians to abandon their commitment to their patient.

Health care today requires the interaction of many caregivers including increasing government oversight, invasion of managed-care regulation, and more significant liability risk.

The culture changes increased frustration due to a perceived loss of autonomy among physicians.

Constructive clinical behavior represents a persistent threat to patient safety and a response that interferes with the ability of others to carry out their duties efficiently, and that undermines the patient confidence in the hospital or another member of the health care team.

Health care provider disbelieving includes intimidation that suppresses input from the other members of the health care team and backlash against a team member.

The behavior can directly impact patient safety in several ways initially safe medication practices experience with evidence of intimidation indicating that nurses frequently do not protect patient–physician when necessary due to past abusive behavior.

Physician adherence to the core values of the medical profession is essential in creating a culture of professionalism and safety. This responsibility goes beyond the basic premise of professionalism; it is committed to the patient.

Efficient systems required an ethical behavior and as an actual component of the professional conduct, they also have been instrumental in introducing safety self-regulation and professional responsibility to establish and enforce standards in most cases.

The organization emphasized the importance of developing a culture with all the members of the health care team. Collaboratively and respectfully reviewing each other's performance and often inputting into team decisions, regardless of power in rank, is a strategy to promote professional behavior and patient safety – an essential step in establishing this fundamental change to health care culture.

Nevertheless, a destructive physician can choose alternatives to violating the principle of safety; along with the code of conduct, there must be a well-designed plan for monitoring compliance with the system – more explicitly referring to professional responsibility.

Medical Profession

Gruen et al. summarize the four characteristics of our profession:

1. A monopoly over the use of specialized knowledge.
2. Relative autonomy in practice and the privilege of self-regulation.
3. Altruistic service to individuals and society.
4. Responsibility for maintaining and expanding professional knowledge and skills. An additional characteristic of a profession is the responsibility to teach its specialized expertise to the public as well as to future practitioners.

These principles are explicitly applied to the three learned professions of divinity, law, and medicine as well as to the military occupation.

The work of the physician is to apply mastery of specialized knowledge, judgment, and skills in service to society. In return, the organization gives the business the privilege of self-regulation, autonomy in practice, and significant financial reward.

What Are the Goals?

1. Demonstrating commitment to ethical principles regarding care, confidentiality, informed consent, and business practices.
2. Showing sensitivity and responsiveness to patients' culture, age, gender, and disabilities according to the Accreditation Council for Graduate Medical Education (ACGME), 1999.

Professionalism Principles

Professionalism principles are based on the principles of the primacy of patient welfare, autonomy, and social justice. It involves the professional responsibilities of

- Competence.
- Honesty.
- Patient confidentiality.
- Appropriate relationships with patients.

Commitment to the Patient: Message and Trust

A commitment to the patient is not only a contract based on the clinical scenario, it is also building a relationship with your patient similar to building one with your colleagues. Unfortunately, as professionals, we need to be careful with many details of our communication such as the elements of the message. When people listen, they do not just listen, they interpret. Out of the message, they grab the following percentages:

- Words–7%
- Tone of voice–38%
- Non-verbal–55%

It is unfair, but it is the reality of the daily life to which we are exposed. It is a tough road to get to trust.

Trust can be built differently by making a message and then expressing the content based on the knowledge of the physician. These are the points of the professionalism that the patient trusts:

- Professionalism is related to patient satisfaction.
- Patients are likely to follow through when they trust the physician.
- Patients are more likely to stay with a physician regarded as professional.
- There is a relationship between physician excellence and professionalism.

The physician must practice to maintain his level of clinical expertise and level of personal excellence. The latter requires a daily review of the following:

- Altruism
- Accountability
- Duty
- Honor and integrity
- Respect
- Commitment to life-long learning

According to an article from JAMA, Epstein[1] defines the latter as "the habitual & judicious use of communication, knowledge, technical skills, clinical reasoning, emotions, values, and reflection in daily practice for the benefit of the individual and community being served."

Assessment of Professionalism

How do we assess professionalism? Here are some tools on which to base our measures, which are the primary requirements expected from the society and the systems:

- Essential and representative expectations per specialty
- Efficient, cognitive, behavioral outcomes
  Additionally, there are five types of relationships the physicians must maintain:
  1. Patient
  2. Society
  3. Another physician
  4. Health care system
  5. Self

There are different types and typology of measurements of professionals, either from institution or peers:

- University of California, San Francisco (UCSF) physician ship evaluation form
- Peer evaluation
- Self-evaluation
- Close and personal observations
- American Board of Internal Medicine (ABIM) scale to measure Professor attitudes and behaviors in medical education
- ACGME website
- Hickson codes, which divided patient complaints by coding them into six categories of professional behavior[2]
- Holleran Chart's abstraction protocol
- Chart reviewed for evidence that ethical issues were addressed[3]

Another method of measurement is reviewing recordings such as videotapes of interactions with patients rated using nine item checklists.[4]

Another is evaluation by an observer like in the Stern Value Code, where professional behaviors observed by trained observers using 37 qualitative codes.[5]

A cognitive test was also administered. Among those used was the Barry Challenges to Professionalism Questionnaire, which included the following:

- Six vignettes portraying challenges to medical professionalism
- With no information about reliability
- Sensitive to different levels of experience

It is also common to use surveys and ratings both indirectly created or created according to the Musik 360° Evaluation, which includes a form filled out using a

26-item checklist by therapists, social workers, case managers, others.[6] Another one is the Wake Forest Physician Trust Scale, which involves instead patients who rate ten items measuring physician professionalism.[7]

The UCSF created a professional curriculum (UCSF professionalism curriculum) that evaluated attributes of a developing physician such as:

- Reliability and responsibility
- Respect/rapport with patients
- Relations with preceptor/support staff
- Motivation and maturity
- Flexibility
- Initiative and self-directed learning

Measures of Competence and Deterioration

Global competence is usually inferred from a sum of measurements in specific areas or fields. Even in these areas, it is impossible to measure "total" skills as it applies to an area. There are, however, a variety of surrogates or proxies and some indirect measures which allow us to define levels of competence within specific specialties. When taken together, these surrogates can provide an acceptable overall evaluation of an individual's ability. Because these proxies all vary regarding training, outcome, and experience, the competencies are specified for residency training under the auspices of graduate medical education and are overseen by ACGME.

A commitment to professional competence is inherently linked to aging and retirement. Deterioration of cognitive, sensory, and psychomotor function with age has obvious implications for patient care as they impact technical and diagnostic skills. These physiologic, cognitive, and behavioral deteriorations have been eloquently summarized by Greenfield.

The *physiologic decline* can include arthritis, diminished flexibility, increased muscle fatigue in combination with diminished muscle mass, decreased exercise tolerance, reduced ability of auditory sensation, and visual deterioration.

Cognitive deteriorations include lengthened memory-retrieval time and word-name blocking.

Behavioral deteriorations include a decline in motivation, creativity, and stress-management ability. Functional decline occurs very slowly, and therefore, may not be recognized by an individual or by an individual's colleagues.

While these functions deteriorate, technology continues to advance, providing another barrier to maintaining competence as the physician tries to keep up with technological innovations.

Maintenance of professional competence boils down to *self-assessment*. The most straightforward measure is to ask yourself if you would allow someone like you – with your current knowledge, skill set, and judgment – to take care of your parent, your child, or yourself. "This above all; to thine own self be true: And it must follow, as the Night the Day, Thou canst not then be false to any man" (William Shakespeare, *Hamlet*). In the same manner, we physicians must be committed to being truthful to ourselves and to our patients.

Notes

1. Epstein, J. M. 2002. Defining and assessing professional competence. *JAMA*, 287(2): 226–35.
2. Hickson, G. B. et al. 2002. Patient complaints and malpractice risk. *JAMA*, 287(22): 2951–7.
3. Holloran, S. D. et al. 1995. An educational intervention in the surgical intensive care unit to improve ethical decisions. *Surgery*, 118(2): 298–299.
4. Beckman, H. et al. 1990. Measurement and improvement of humanistic skills in first-year trainees. *J Gen Intern Med*, 5(1):42–5.
5. Stern, D. T. 1996. Values on call: a method for assessing the teaching of professionalism. *Academic Medicine*, 71(10): 37–39.
6. Barry, D. et al. 2000. Common issues in medical professionalism: Room to grow. *AM J Med*, 108(2): 136–142.
7. Hall, M. A. et al. 2002. Measuring patients' trust in their primary care providers. *Med Care Res Rev*, 59(3): 293–318.

Suggested Reading

1. American College of Surgeons. Accessed at URL: http://www.efacs.org.
2. Bunkin, I. A. 1983. When does a surgeon retire? *JAMA*, 250(6): 757–8.
3. Cruess, R. L., S. R. Cruess, and S. E. Johnston. 2000. Professionalism: An ideal to be sustained. *Lancet*, 356(9224): 156–9.
4. Cruess, S. R., S. Johnston, and R. L. Cruess. 2002. Professionalism for medicine: Opportunities and obligations. *Med J Aust*, 177(4): 208–211.
5. Greenfield, L. J. 1994. Farewell to surgery. *J Vasc Surg*, 19(1): 6–14.
6. Gruen, R. L., Arya, J., Cosgrove, E. M., Cruess, R. L., Cruess, S. R., Eastman, A. B., Fabri, P. J., Friedman, P., Kirksey, T. D., Kodner, I. J. and Lewis, F. R. 2003. Professionalism in surgery. *J Am Coll Surg*, 197(4): 605–8.
7. Hart, M. J. 2007. An inexplicable bond. Pacific Coast Surgical Association Presidential Address 2007. *Arch Surg*, In Press.
8. Mathers, N. J., Challis, M.C., Howe, A.C., and Field, N.J. 1999. Portfolios in continuing medical education—effective and efficient? *Med Educ*, 33(7): 521–30.
9. Miscall, B. G., R. K. Tompkins, and L. J. Greenfield. 1996. ACS survey explores retirement and the surgeon. *Bull Am Coll Surg*, 81(12): 18–25.
10. Reznick, R., Regehr, G., MacRae, H., Martin, J., and McCulloch, W. 1997. Testing technical skill via an innovative "bench station" examination. *Am J Surg*, 173(3): 226–30.
11. The Oxford English Dictionary. Accessed at URL: http://dictionary.oed.com.

Ethics Summary Table

How to Reach Professionalism

Competence
Honesty
Patient confidentiality
Appropriate relationships with patients
Altruism
Accountability
Duty
Honor and integrity
Respect
Commitment to life-long learning
Extended life of continuous medical education
Keep up our competences

Chapter 5

Sexual Harassment

Quid Pro Quo

Title VII of the Civil Rights Act, issued by the Supreme Court, defines types of sexual harassment

1. Quid pro quo: Job security, advancement, or benefits secondary to sexual favors.
2. This type includes unwelcome sexual advances, requests for sexual favors, or physical or verbal conduct of a sexual nature related directly or implicitly to employment.

The 2016 study, published in the *Journal of the American Medical Association*[1] was one of the first to give a more in-depth idea of sexual harassment in health care. Investigators interviewed 1,066 men and women. They were all physicians, average age 43, with an award toward their careers by the National Institute of Health. Despite their young age, they had already experienced gender bias, gender advantage, and sexual harassment.

The study showed that 70% of women had perceived gender bias in the academic environment, while 66% had experienced it personally. 22% of men reported that they had viewed gender bias, and 10% had personally experienced it.

Unacceptable Accepted Practice

With women comprising more than half of the health care staff in the United States, the high percentage of sexual harassment in the workplace is a massive cause for concern. The Bureau of Labor Statistics published an updated list of labor force statistics in February 2016. According to their findings, women comprise 78.5% of the 20,077 employees who work in health care. More specifically, of 6,698 hospital employees, women constitute 78.5%.

Sexual harassment is frequent in the health care industry. The power dynamics in some large institutions can be quite complicated with multiple departments and multiple supervisors and levels of authority.

The old-school idea that it was acceptable for doctors or those in authority to denigrate or abuse (verbally or otherwise) health care personnel, such as nurses, is just no longer tenable; however, sexual harassment of health care workers by physicians remains a problem.

Harassment by patients is also unacceptable, but the patient's condition must be considered when planning an intervention.

For example, if a patient has dementia, he or she may not be responsible for their behavior.

However, the employee and supervisor or other team members should work together to find a way to prevent or manage the offending behavior.[2]

Policies

Health care facilities should have strategies in place for dealing with outright sexual harassment from patients, and these procedures should be followed.

If no such policy exists, then health care workers should request a plan be written.

Harassment should always be documented in the appropriate incident report and reported to a supervisor. In some cases, patients have been sexually harassed by staff. In this case, anyone who observes this or receives a report about it from a patient must document and report this harassment as well.

Hostile Working Environment

A hostile work environment can be defined as inappropriate behavior so pervasive and severe that it permeates the workplace and interferes with the individual's ability to carry out the duties of the job.

In the same environment, the message is clear without any question about possible "quid pro quo."

In other situations, the harassment is more subtle and not apparent right away. The problems are revealed when the work environment becomes so difficult to sustain that the "harassed" person has no choice but to resign.

The psychological effect of the harassment is not readily evident at the beginning, but in the long term, is harder to sustain than the verbal or the apparent one pushing the employee to resign. Work under such conditions is difficult and can result in problems such as drinking and using drugs.

Harassment is now also considered as aberrant behavior that makes people uncomfortable. We think that this leaves too much open and that it needs to be defined and regulated; otherwise, everyone can complain about this one day or another.

We would like to follow up with court cases reported by the American Nurses Association (ANA) as an example of same legal action from courts. Most quid pro quo cases also include a hostile work environment.[2]

Court cases: Female v Verizon Communications, Inc. A female employee claimed that she was regularly called a "bitch" and "stupid" and was denied equipment, access to public restrooms, and overtime, subjected to discipline for acts commonly completed by men who were not disciplined, and forced to use bathrooms without locks.

The court agreed this constituted a hostile work environment.

*Female v Forklift System*s. A female worked as a manager and was repeatedly insulted by the company president, who disparaged her gender and made sexual innuendos and offensive statements about her to other employees.

The woman complained to the president about his behavior, and he promised to stop but resumed harassment again. She resigned and filed suit. The trial court ruled against her because she had not suffered injury (such as a nervous breakdown). However, the Supreme Court overturned this ruling, stating that a hostile environment need not be so severe as to cause severe psychological injury. This is an example of quid pro quo constructive discharge and a hostile work environment.

Male v Sundowner Offshore Services (1998). A male oilrig worker was harassed by male co-workers and was subjected to humiliating actions, including being held down and sodomized with a bar of soap. When he reported the harassment to the supervisor, he was called an insulting name and no action was taken.

He resigned and filed suit. The lower court dismissed the lawsuit because he was a male, but the Supreme Court overturned this ruling, stating that the sexual harassment laws apply to men and same-sex harassment. This is an example of quid pro quo constructive discharge and a hostile work environment.

Type of Harassments

Several forms of harassment in health care are reported. We chose the description from the American Nurses Association from their meeting in Chicago:[2]

Verbal (Spoken or Written)

- Offensive teasing
- Joking
- Questioning
- Suggestive remarks or sounds. Terms of endearment, such as "honey," "sweetie," or "hunk"
- Requests for sexual favors
- Whistling
- Catcalls
- Inappropriate emails, letters, memos, telephone calls, etc.
- Comments about appearance, clothing
- Threats
- Spreading rumors about a person's personal or sexual life

Non-Verbal

- Sexual gestures (licking, making hand signals, eating provocatively)
- Winking or leering/looking inappropriately at a person's body or body parts
- Blocking a person's path, following the person
- Giving personal gifts
- Visual: Sexual exposure including "flashing" or "mooning"
- Offensive pictures, pornography, posters, pin-ups, etc.
- Offensive screensavers
- Physical touching, raping, brushing against the body, patting, stroking, hugging, kissing, caressing, etc.
- Massaging the neck or shoulders
- Psychological repeated undesired social invitations, proposals, or contact resulting in anxiety and stress

Who Needs to Watch?

The question is who needs to watch over this critical issues? The answer is simple. Everybody.

- Managers
- Supervisors
- Associates (including employed physicians)
- Non-associate physicians
- Customers
- Vendors and visitors

All of the roles mentioned above are in charge of watching for unwanted behavior toward all class of people, woman, veterans, disabled, children, foreign seniors, etc.

Sexually harassing conduct requires some particular attention because it is often hard to define. It can include behavior between people of the same sex as well. It can consist of

- The unwelcome conduct of a sexual nature
- Sexual advances
- Requests for sexual favors
- Other verbal, visual, or physical behavior with a sexual aim
- Comments
- Touching
- Teasing
- Joking
- Intimidation

We are aware that conduct which might be offensive to some individuals might be considered inoffensive to others. We are also mindful that not all conduct of a sexual nature amounts to illegal sexual harassment. However, we believe it is essential to put a stop to harassing behavior before is late. Too late is when the action interferes with the daily job and with the psychological health of the person and employee.

Is There an Antiharassment Policy?

There are options for people who have been on the receiving end or witnessed harassing conduct. These are outlined in the following antiharassment policies from Wheaton Hospital, Iowa[3]

1. Approach the alleged harasser and ask him/her to stop the offensive activity immediately. They may not know how you or others feel. Of course, this step is not required if it makes you feel uncomfortable or is not useful.
2. If you want to make a formal complaint and have your complaint investigated, you must promptly bring the matter to the attention of the Human Resources Director for Wheaton Franciscan Healthcare-IA.
3. Human Resources will take prompt action to assure that your complaint is impartially and thoroughly investigated. Confidentiality will be maintained to the best extent possible during the investigation.
4. If an investigation reveals that this policy has been violated, Human Resources will take prompt and appropriate corrective action reasonably designed to stop the harassment and prevent recurrences, which may include discipline or discharge of the harasser.

Retaliating or discriminating against someone for complaining about harassing conduct or cooperating in an investigation is also a violation of this policy that can result in discipline or discharge. If you believe you have been retaliated against, report this fact immediately to Human Resources.

How To Report Harrassment

Since most harassment has been against women, the American Nurses Association was the first to raise the issues and develop a way to report the harassment.

In their publication on sexual harassment,[2] the association outlines a way of reporting these issues as described in the following points from their course.

1. Employers are required to take reasonable care to prevent sexual harassment and take reasonable care to promptly correct sexual harassment once it occurs.
2. It's important to remember that the employer cannot be held responsible for behavior about which the employer is unaware. This means that the employee being harassed should always notify the employer (unless there is a reason to fear for their personal safety).
3. If the employer takes appropriate action, such as warning the person doing the harassing, the employer has acted with reasonable care.
4. Additionally, employees should be very clear about the definition of sexual harassment.
5. Employees may choose to go through the employer's complaint process or file a charge with a state fair employment agency or Federal EEOC (Equal Employment Opportunity Commission).
6. Employees may also file a civil suit to ask for damages. Under Federal and most state laws, employees must file a complaint within 180 days of an act of sexual harassment. This may vary somewhat by state laws; for example, California allows 300 days.

Documentation

Consensual behavior is not considered sexual harassment, so the employee must be very clear about saying "No."

If asked for a date, "I already have plans" or "I have a girlfriend" or "I don't like workplace romances" is not the same as "No, I don't want to date."

Laughing uncomfortably at a dirty joke is not the same as saying "I don't want to hear dirty jokes. They make me uncomfortable."

This gives the harassed person the duty to report, otherwise, he/she will be considered complicit to the action.

Report the incidence following employer procedures; the employee should make a formal complaint to the appropriate supervisor in writing, outlining precisely what has occurred and providing evidence or supporting the statement with witnesses as necessary.

Documentation such as a written record is a must. This should include

1. The complaint (the report of the fact)
2. Actions the employer has taken
3. Any responsibility from those who had engaged in harassment
4. All letters, emails, and summaries of telephone conversations or meetings

Documentation is essential in case the complaints will go to legal action.

Conclusion

While some behavior is so clearly offensive that it is blatantly sexual harassment, most behaviors are not. If the action is welcome, it will never escalate to the level of inappropriate behavior, despite company policies.

Passive acceptance is a way to accept the behavior. Sensibility and sensitivity of the issues need to be implemented, not just with a mere slide reading at the time of the orientation but with continuing education about the problems and how to solve them.

The most important thing is that employees need to feel protected from the offender and not be afraid of any repercussions, such as losing their job or more.

Protect the victim; this should be the goal for the future.

Notes

1. Jagsi, R. et al. 2016. Sexual harassment and discrimination experiences of academic medical faculty. *JAMA*. 315(19): 2120–2021.
2. Lockwood, W. 2017. Sexual harassment in healthcare. Accessed at URL: http://www.rn.org/courses/coursematerial-236.pdf.
3. Wheaton Franciscan Healthcare. Anti-harassment policy. Accessed at URL: https://www.wheatoniowa.org/webres/File/Anti%20Harassment%20Policy.pdf.

Suggested Reading

1. American Sociological Association 2009, August 13. Female Supervisors More Susceptible To Workplace Sexual Harassment. ScienceDaily. Retrieved February 8, 2011, Accessed at URL: http://www.sciencedaily.com-/releases/2009/08/090810025247.htm.

2. Committee on Pediatric Workforce. 2006, October. Prevention of sexual harassment in the workplace and educational settings. *Pediatrics* 118 (4): 1752–1756. Accessed at URL: http://aappolicy.aappublications.org/cgi/reprint/pediatrics;118/4/1752.pdf.
3. Equal Rights Advocates. 2011 Know your rights: Sexual harassment at work. Accessed at URL: http://www.equalrights.org/publications/kyr/shwork.asp.
4. Inappropriate patient behavior tough on nurses. 2005, December 15. MSNBC.com. Accessed at URL: http://www.msnbc.msn.com/id/10484939/ns/healthhealth_care/.

Ethics Summary Table

How to Avoid Sexual Harassment

Avoid quid pro quo

Avoid situations in which denigration or authority can cause mixed feelings

Make the environment available and open

Avoid disturbing sounds, joking, pictures, and computer content

Implement a no threat policy

Everybody is responsible for watching for and reporting sexual harassment

Set up a policy and training

PHYSICIAN PROFESSIONAL RELATIONSHIP

Chapter 6

Patient–Physician Relationship

Ethical analysis is accomplished by gathering facts and asking such questions as what are the issues, who is involved, and what are the beliefs, values, and opinions of the involved individuals? After this analysis, a decision can be made.

Since Hippocrates, we have made some advancements in our moral thinking, but it is striking how many of his original moral precepts hold up today. The complexity of modern medical care has brought forth new and complex issues regarding end-of-life care and parental concerns, among others. In the future, more ethical teachings and ethically based understanding need to be taught in medical school and during residency.

Principles of Ethics for Physicians Taking Care of Patients

The medical profession is directly related to ethical principles, developed primarily for the benefit of the patient.

Some definitions of basic ethics are the following:

1. *The principle of proportionality.* Treatment is mandatory to the extent that it will confer more significant benefits than burdens upon the patient.
2. *Autonomy.* The right of a competent individual to make decisions.
3. *Beneficence.* The duty to provide actions which provide a higher balance of good over harm; "First, to do no harm."
4. *Paternalism.* Beneficence has priority over autonomy.

5. *Nonmaleficence.* Duty to refrain from causing damage.
6. *Justice.* Receiving compensation or resolution to which one is entitled.

The principles of ethics for physicians could be summarized in the following nine points adopted from the American Medical Association (AMA) policies.[1]

1. Respect human life and the dignity of every individual;
2. Refrain from supporting or committing crimes against humanity and condemn all such acts;
3. Treat the sick and injured with competence and compassion and without prejudice;
4. Apply knowledge and skills – regardless of risk;
5. Protect privacy and confidentiality;
6. Work freely with colleagues to discover new medical principles;
7. Develop and promote advances in medicine;
8. Educate the public about present and future threats to health; and
9. Teach and mentor those who follow the physician.

JCAHO's Sentinel Event Advisory Group, through an intensive process of review of all past sentinel event recommendations, developed the following set of six National Patient Safety Goals, for use by health care organizations:

1. Improve the accuracy of patient identification
2. Improve the effectiveness of communication among caregivers
3. Improve the safety of using high-alert medications
4. Eliminate wrong-site, wrong-patient, wrong-procedure surgery
5. Improve the safety of using infusion pumps
6. Improve the effectiveness of clinical alarm systems

Doctor–Patient Relationship

This relationship can be divided into the following four sections:

1. *Fiduciary relationship.* The physician is a trustee in respect to confidence and trust and must promote and protect the patients' interests beyond the scope of any regular business contract.
2. Care is initiated by the patient's consent and sustained by the patient accepting the physician's recommendations.
3. The patient may terminate the relationship at will.

4. The physician must give adequate notice to terminating care and provide help finding another physician.

Informed Consent

Informed consent is a shared decision-making process that requires the physician to disclose an adequate amount of information, including alternative strategies for diagnosis and treatment, with the risks and benefits of each outlined. The physician has an ethical responsibility to make reasonable efforts to ensure the patient's comprehension by asking questions.

The elements of informed consent include:

1. Benefits versus risk;
2. Chances for success or failure;
3. Sharing the goals of treatment; and
4. Alternative therapies and their chances of success or failure and their benefits vs. risks.

Patient–Physician Collaborations

It is no longer appropriate for the physician to be the patient's decision maker. We must present medical facts that help ensure that patients, and their families, are informed. We can make recommendations, but it is the patient's decision. There must be collaboration with patients and families. Early on, after an illness or injury, the discussion should be initiated as to the goals and wishes of the patient with specific emphasis on preference for life-sustaining measures. We must remember to provide information in lay terms as well as ask and invite questions. We must ensure consistency between discussions and provide recommendations based on medically achieved goals. There must be open discourse about disagreements, and all should be done before death is imminent.

Any time physicians finds themselves at odds with the family in a way that cannot be solved quickly and efficiently, then the bioethics committee should be urgently consulted.

Ethics provides us principles, but quite often judgment is required for each patient scenario with each treated individually. We must monitor these four principles as we approach these difficult situations: (1) respect the capacity and autonomy of individuals to make their own decisions and choices; (2) do no harm (nonmaleficence); (3) prevent and treat pain and suffering; and (4) act fairly and resolve dilemmas. One's character and experiences become the moral guide. We must always remember the secret to the care of a patient is caring for that patient.

Continuum of Care

Continuum of care implies that the treatment does not have a visible end; it is ongoing care where the outcome becomes less and less predictable, and most likely, indicates the end of life. There are situations where therapy may cross the line from potential survival to maintaining signs of being purely down to medicine and machines. The physician more than likely will be dealing not only with the patient but with family and friends. More than likely physicians will find themselves interpreting living wills and advanced directives. A legal guardian or appropriate next of kin will most often be the person with whom discussions occur.

Relationship at the End of Life

We must remember that a doctor's relationship with a patient is fiduciary. We should always serve the patient's best interest over our own.

Once a physician determines that care is pointless, decisions may involve withdrawal of care or withholding of therapy. Futility is an action that will fail and that ought not to be attempted. The discussion surrounding such choices should outline the fact that there is no set right or wrong way to alter end-of-life care.

The clinical findings must be documented and discussed in understandable lay terms. These findings should be communicated to family and friends as to how they should interact with the patient, encouraging touching, talking, etc.

There should be discussion as to what treatment and devices will be removed and what treatment will not be started. If the ventilator is an issue, extubation may allow the patient to talk if they are conscious and have minimal secretions. A discussion should occur as to what to expect – agonal respirations, changes in the monitor, etc. It is also essential to explain that time of death is impossible to predict and may take what seems like a long time. In the end, no matter how involved the discussions are in preparing the family, always expect significant grief and even the possibility of frustration or anger that at times may be directed at the physician or other members of the health care team.

Discussions of ethics, especially when dealing with the continuance of care or withdrawal of care, should have a set environment.

1. *Privacy*: The physician–patient relationship should be conducted in a private area away from other patients and visitors and the rumble of the hospitals. These decisions are a significant shock for a family member, and we need to set the scene most respectfully.
2. *Compassion*. The physician should sit at eye level and should try to have support for the person making decisions in the form of one or two individuals with which they feel comfortable (ministers, close friends, or members of the family). The physician should set the stage for a discussion with appropriate opening remarks, true statements regardless of whether the news is good or bad.

3. *Allow time.* Silence and listening are essential adjuncts to use – it helps those representing the patient to digest the information. It is also necessary for the physician to instill hope, not that a cure can occur but that the health care team won't abandon them.

Advance Directives

An adult patient with decision-making capacity generally may refuse any treatment unless the refusal endangers public health, or an unborn or very young, dependent child guaranteed under rights of privacy doctrine. Denial of treatment is not evidence per se of decreased capacity or incompetence. When the physician disagrees with the patient on a prognosis, he or she should transfer care to another person.

Advance directives are divided into the following:

1. Living wills are instructional directives that give specific details or a general statement of wishes.
2. Durable power of attorney is a legal process that appoints a health care representative (proxy directive); the health care representative uses substituted judgment to decide what the patient would have settled in these circumstances.
3. Advance directive legislation – basic and principles of the state where you are treated.
4. Courts may determine on advance directives using the best interest concept based on what a "typical patient" would want in the same circumstances.

Barriers to broader use of advance directives include:

1. Advance directives are not read and discussed by the physician early in the course of treatment;
2. The health care proxy is unable or unwilling to follow or support the instruction directive;
3. The physician is guided by the family regardless of the advance directive of patient;
4. The advance directive is not honored in certain circumstances (out-of-hospital CPR); and
5. The advance directive was prepared by a lawyer without appropriate medical understanding, which can be dangerous.

Family Belief and Religions

Belief or religion almost always plays some role during situations where the continuum of care has reached a point where the discussion of end of life begins.

Christianity, Judaism, and Islam all have in common that they expect the medical team to avoid:

1. The thought that we could end life.
2. Vitalism – that our life on earth has absolute value and all means must be taken for its preservation.
3. They all agree that the health care team should not impose life-sustaining therapies when the burden of treatment far exceeds the benefit or where such therapies will merely prolong the dying process.
4. They support physicians speaking openly about death and dying with the patients, being frank about the limits of medical care.

Everybody expects us to work hard to prolong life and never overtly take life, but recognize that there are limits, when treatment should be withdrawn or withheld. Some religions have some official statement about artificial nutrition and possible life-prolonging activities. Also, they have reports concerning when it is appropriate to remove these types of supports. From a religious perspective, they feel the health care team's mission is to defend human dignity and be responsible stewards of health care resources. We must not stand in the way of ensuring pastoral care for the spiritual needs of our patients.

Note

1. AMA. 2001. Declaration of professional responsibility. Accessed at URL: https://www.cms.org/uploads/Declaration-of-Professional-Responsibility.pdf.

Suggested Reading

1. AMA. 2018. Physician-Patient Relationship. Accessed at URL: https://www.ama-assn.org/delivering-care/patient-physician-relationships. AMA. 2012. AMA Pledged To Educate The Public And Polity* – "Humanity Is Our Patient." August 29. Accessed at URL:
2. Ballard, K. 2003. Patient safety: A shared responsibility. *Patient Safety*, 8(3). Accessed at URL: http://www.nursingworld.org/MainMenuCategories/ANAMarketplace/ANAPeriodicals/OJIN/TableofContents/Volume82003/No3Sept2003/PatientSafety.html
3. District of Columbia Durable Power of Attorney Law. Accessed at URL: http://statelaws.findlaw.com/dc-law/district-of-Columbia-durable-power-of-attorney-laws.html.
4. DiversityInc Staff. 2008. Things to Say to People with Disabilities. July 21. Accessed at URL: http://www.diversityinc.com/things-not-to-say/things-to-say-to-people-with-disabilities.

5. Goold, S. D., and M. Lipkin, Jr. 1999. The Doctor-Patient Relationship. Challenges, Opportunities, and Strategies. Susan Dorr Goold, MD, MHSA, MA and Mack Lipkin, Jr., MD *J Gen Intern Med,*. 1999 Jan; 14(Suppl 1): S26–S33.
6. http://www.healthcommentary.org/2012/08/29/ama-pledged-to-educate-the-public-and.
7. Physician-Patient Relationship. Accessed at URL: https://physicians.uslegal.com/physician-patient-relationships/.
8. Social Determinants of Health Initiative Social Justice Pledge. Accessed at URL: https://www.pdx.edu/social-determinants-health/sites/www.pdx.edu.social-determinants-health.

Ethics Summary Table

How to Build Patient–Physician Relationship

Explain the value of the treatment
Balance beneficence with good judgment
Leave the patient time to decide
Respect human life and your patient
Use compassion and competence
Educate the patient and their family
Clear and written informed consent
Always use a witness
Expect the patient to contribute
The family needs to be part of your team, particularly in an end-of-life situation
Check for an advance directive or make one
Respect beliefs and religion

Chapter 7

Commitment to Honesty and Trust

The relationship with the health care worker and the patient is grounded in respect for trust and ethical principles.

Physician Limitations

- The patient needs to trust a provider.
- The patient is becoming more sophisticated and questions and answers are necessary.
- The government and health organization, therefore, came out with parameters.
- The quality initiative monitors the outcomes.
- Disease and recurrence are monitored and applied to every single physician and hospital organization.

In the hospital there is more scrutiny of:

- Infections
- Surgical complications
- Wrong usage of medication
- False diagnoses
- Readmission

Zero Dashboard

- Is one of the initiatives to decrease problems and complications and give a better quality of care.
- It is imperative nowadays to achieve this which can be done using the computerizing system.

Recognize Limitations

Processes of seniority resulted from the canonical interplay of several factors.

- Increased technical skill
- Preparedness and cognitive ability
- Recognizing our limitations in different contexts brings efficiency
- Training in school
- Training after school
- Hospital training
- Follow your and peer progression
- Follow the quality of your work

Engage in the Relationship

Trust is defined as the willingness of the party to be vulnerable to the actions of another party. But who is monitoring?

I tell the patient that whatever operation or steps during the procedure would be the same ones I would want to be performed on myself or my loved ones. That usually reassures the patient and is one of the moments that they will recount at a subsequent office visit.

One way we are led to "truth" is by following level one evidence. The postoperative drain in the gallbladder bed was a "truth" for many years. Eventually level one evidence and surgical expediency led surgeons to abandon that drain for most cholecystectomies and many other types of surgery. Ethics should not be used to pronounce those kinds of surgical maneuvers excellent or bad.

The "payors" force the decision tree for legitimizing and popularizing a new or different treatment. The decision to perform a given operation or use a device, hinges on the probability of reimbursement, even before we have to deal with any ethical issue. The other side of the equation is that the long time it takes to abandon a procedure proven to be dangerous can be much longer than the time it takes to approve the system.

Honesty

So, understanding the importance of honesty is the most important outcome in any societies in the medical profession.

Advocacy for patient interest and welfare required the following competencies:

- Having a good practice
- Interpersonal skills
- Making the correct decision
- Avoiding mistakes

We need in our heart and soul to reassure the patient that procedures, diagnostic tests, and clinical pathways are of a high standard of care because we know our hospital or department can always perform a root cause analysis of any complication to try to prevent reoccurrence and a malpractice review. The problem is how often the cause analysis is used? How often are complications filtered out of any form of discussion, and openly discussed, without any possible backlash? That analysis activates the transparency ethic.

Patient Autonomy

The patient should preserve their autonomy. They should have the last decision and words on their treatment, and they should be able to do their research. Requesting more information or a second opinion should be the norm and not the exception.

The watch is turning, swinging from the physician–health care worker decision to absolute patient autonomy, and the emphasis on the relationship and trust building is becoming more critical.

Patients seeking medical care place themselves in a precarious condition – to place their lives in the hand of somebody else is what the patient does by going to see a physician.

Therefore, they need to weigh and balance their understanding of the procedure and its consequences.

Patient autonomy is defined as the independence of choices and the availability of extra sources. This is informed consent.

From all these subjects we can extrapolate some conclusions and directions:

- Medicare, Medicaid, and VA placed emphasis on the road justice and treatment of the patient.
- Many physicians practice day by day ethics more than anybody else probably in any profession.
- Honesty is the act of transferring medicine fairness in all human interaction.

- The potential benefit of disclosing information outweighs the possible harmful consequences as they would increase emphasis on patient autonomy an equal partnership.
- The patient requires information to decide.
- It is challenging to keep the truth away from the patient in modern times because there is a lot all web information and basic knowledge available.
- In Europe and Latin America, the family can ask not to release information to protect the patient psychological event in case of terminal illness.
- This is something to discuss with the family with the power of attorney.

Patient autonomy strives toward equality in this partnership:

- A significant change in law and medicine will change the relationship.
- The first was the requirement for a simple consent for the treatment of a specifically invasive procedure.

The landmark decision was reached in 1914 when Judge Benjamin Cardozo stated "every human being of adult years and sound mind has a right to determine what shall be done. No one has to perform any procedure without the patient consent." This was part of a verdict in New York Hospital.

Global Trust

- Honesty, which is telling the truth and avoiding intentional false hope
- Confidentiality, which is a proper use of the sensitive information
- Global trust, which is the soul of confidence or aspect that combine elements from some or all of the other dimensions

Building Trust

- The central theme of building trust is honesty and trustworthiness brought on a professional organizational and an individual level.
- How can human pain relate to trust?
- The initial development of trust is the meeting between the physician and the patient ending by exposing all the issues that need to be presented, such as what it is natural, what the problem is, and what the future treatment will be.
- The trust means that you continue to talk to the family to be sure that everyone is on the same page.
- The initial step is based on the global and professional respect.

- Several studies have shown that the deciding factor for trust in the physician is the interpersonal relationship between the physician and the patient, which is usually established before surgery.
- The same approach applies to the nurse; the relationship is to be built in the first few hours of taking care of the patient.
- The physician and the nurse need to be present to explain any consent needed in detail.

Errors

- The error may not result in the adverse event but can still be troubling to the patient.
- The American Medical Association states that the physician should deal honestly and openly with the patient at all times.
- At the international level, there was a lot of initiative in Australia/United Kingdom on the ways to decrease the medical error to talk to the patient.
- In the United States in 2005, the same time as the campaign was launched in Australia and the United Kingdom, Senators Hillary Clinton and Barack Obama sponsored a bill – The National Medical Error Disclosing and Compensation Act.

Disclosure

- Disclosure would increase the likelihood of malpractice action.
- This concern has done much to impede the flow of information to patient and family.
- Despite this, it is now clear that the patient wants to know about all errors that cause them harm.
- Another study showed that the patient would be less likely to seek legal advice when the error was disclosed.
- Nurse leader–hospital administration need to be involved in the revealing process and offer the emotional support to patient and family should any necessary support should be needed.
- The patient should also be told what measure would be taken to assure the scenario does not occur in the future to another patient.

Legal

The legal aspect of the medical profession every physician or health care practitioner are concerned with, to some degree, is to avoid involvement of medical malpractice lawsuit.

Protecting the patient from harm is no doubt a primary concern at the foundation of every medical practice of any professional. It should include a plan to reduce the risk by utilizing protocols standard, standard care, and best practice develop skills for effective patient – physician communication; this type of model can help reduce the number of medical errors or anticipated outcomes that occur in assisting the physician to efficiently manage this event.

Transparency

- Studies overwhelming show that apologies and transparent disclosure is the best risk management tool.
- The standard required health care organization to disclose unanticipated outcomes of care or treatment for their patient and, when appropriate, to their family with issues of concern, including unexpected results.
- A sense of compassion – an understanding of the pain after the apology. The physician needs to practice what they will say and not practice the same thing over and over again.
- Second, a responsible, independent practitioner knows always to explain the outcome of any treatment or procedure to the patient, and when appropriate, to the patient's family.
- Whenever findings are significantly different from anticipated results, this can spark some controversies because not all adverse consequences are caused by medical error or negligence. The first step must be a collaborative effort with the family and the patient, and a structured plan of action can help assure complete and timely disclosure of the event.
- The standard does not require documentation of exposure but to avoid any doubt, a team approach of having more than one witness during the explanation.
- The AMA has similar ethics requirements as part of their code of ethics, and its fundamental ethics require that the physician should, at all times, be honest and open with their patient.
- Situations occasionally occur in which a patient suffers a significant medical complication. In the situation, the physician is ethically required to inform the patient of all facts necessary to ensure understanding of what has occurred.
- The independence that should be afforded to the patient or the amount of information required to make an informed health care decision.

Arrogance

- Arrogant, inattentive physicians are more likely to have a lawsuit filed against them not necessarily because of the outcome of a medical mix-up but because of an unsatisfactory feeling.

- Communication includes the consideration from disclosure; sympathetic concern and respect are things that everyone expects.
- One of the most effective forms of communication is apologizing. An apology needs to be an admission of fault or negligence but should also be a demonstration of compassion and understanding of what the apology is for. "I'm sorry" may be a standard phrase but it needs to be phrased in a way that means it.
- Physician's ability to recognize, regret, take responsibility for, and remedy must always be visible when an apology is appropriate; so fear, frustration, or anger should be placed aside.
- An apology should be considered. Keep in mind that an excuse should not be reserved solely for the medical mix-up but is also appropriate for situations of less severity, such as a long wait before an appointment, behavior by staff, delay in returning a telephone call, or delay in answering when the nurses call into the room.

Suggested Reading

1. ABIM. 2018. ABIM Foundation Principles. Accessed at URL: http://abimfoundation.org/what-we-do/physician-charter.
2. Blendon, R. J., J. M. Benson, and J. O. Hero. 2014. Public Trust in Physicians — U.S. Medicine in International Perspective, October 23. *N Engl J Med* 371: 1570–2. Accessed at URL: http://www.nejm.org/doi/full/10.1056/NEJMp1407373.
3. Hunt, M. 1989. Body and Mind; Patients' Rights. March 5. Accessed at URL: http://www.nytimes.com/1989/03/05/magazine/body-and-mind-patients-rights.html.
4. Medical Professionalism Project: ABIM Foundation. 2002. Medical Professionalism in the New Millennium: A Physician Charter. *Project of the ABIM Foundation, ACP–ASIM Foundation, and European Federation of Internal Medicine*, February 5. Accessed at URL: http://annals.org/aim/fullarticle/474090/medical-professionalism-new-millennium-physician-charter.
5. State of Maine. 2018. Rights and Legal Issues – Involuntary Commitment. Accessed at URL: http://www.maine.gov/dhhs/samhs/mentalhealth/rights-legal/involuntary/faq/home.html.
6. Thom, D. H.Sabrina T. Wong, David Guzman, A. Wu, J. Penko, C. Miaskowski, and M. Kushel. Physician Trust in the Patient: Development and Validation of a New Measure. *Ann Farm Med* 9(2): 148–54. Accessed at URL: http://www.annfammed.org/content/9/2/148.

Ethics Summary Table

How to Commit to Honesty and Trust

Recognize your limitations
Aim for zero dashboard

Prepare for possible cognitive and physical restrictions
Engage in a trusting relationship with your patient
Make a decision and admit issues and failures
Respect patient's autonomy
Build trust
Disclose interests
Disclose errors
Watch your legal limitations
Be transparent
Avoid arrogance

Chapter 8

Disclosing Medical Errors

"Errare humanum est, perseverare autem diabolicum"

Lucius Annaeus Seneca

Seneca's words in English read "to err is human; to continue in error, diabolical." All physicians, being wise, make mistakes; good physicians minimize the probability of a recurrence. Morbidity and mortality conferences enable all to better future results by learning what might have been done better when an adverse outcome has occurred. Protocols, by standardizing care, effectively reduce the risk of persistent error by having the institution learn from past mistakes either at the system making changes in contracts or at unknown institutions by the simple adoption of protocols in hospitals that have not yet experienced significant errors.

Metrics such as infection rates can be interpreted as a means to adjudge the existence of persistent error. The Center for Medical Services (CMS) mandates data collection, analyses of which partly determine whether physicians are permitted to practice in hospitals and clinics. Although some metrics are specialty specific, others (e.g., criminal medical records, malpractice claims, disruptive behavior) apply to almost all physicians. Hospitals and clinics also have metrics that relate to their performance (e.g., patients are seen or patients that have left without being seen, patient's complaints, appropriate protocol usage for preventable diseases). Reimbursement is now linked to the quality of care metrics, meaning that failure to reach any of a variety of quantitative goals decreases income.

The Impact of Medical Errors

There are estimated to be 98,000 deaths per year due to medical error. This means medical errors are the fifth leading cause of death in the United States. The most common avoidable errors are:

■ Two million hospital-acquired infections/year – 90,000 deaths: (a) Methicillin-resistant *Staphylococcus aureus* infection (MRSA); (b) Vancomycin-resistant *E. coli*; (c) Metronidazole-resistant *Clostridium difficile*
■ Patient falls: 70% of "hospital accidents" – 30% Geriatric patients die within a year of fall.
■ One million pressure sores (decubitus ulcers) and 60,000 related deaths. Medication errors: 400,000 drugs errors among Medicare patients/year.

Cost of treating injuries due to medication error: $3.5 billion/year.
Lethal medication errors have resulted in:

■ Revocation of nursing and physician licenses
■ Charges of "criminal negligent homicide"
■ Media reporting more incidents of adverse outcomes involving nursing care or allegations of nursing negligence or misconduct
■ Increased responsibility, role expansion and scope of practice
■ Expansion of federal and state health care laws
■ Mandatory patient advocacy – especially support of informed decision making

Miscommunication Number 1!

Likely, the most common and preventable errors stem from miscommunication. Computerized drug administration can prevent dosage mistakes. Electronic medical records can preclude reliance on a faulty memory of persons not immediately present. Nurse instructors/clinical educators can correct miscommunication between caregiver and patient, whether due to a lack of attention or communication skill on the part of the physician or a lapse in interest or memory on the part of the patient; written instructions, preferably signed by the patient after such interventions, are essential.

Faulty communication is among the most common underlying causes of medical error and can lead directly to the breakdown of a therapeutic patient–physician relationship. Once this failure occurs, patients become angry. Angry patients who feel they have been treated by defensive, evasive, hostile, arrogant, or inattentive physicians following a medical mishap are more likely to file a lawsuit. This is not necessarily because of the outcome of care but the lack of adequate communication by the physician following the incident.

Communication skills are most important after an adverse outcome. True sympathetic concern by the physician expresses itself in the form of an acknowledgment of the patient's situation and distress.

Demonstrated compassion and understanding, not necessarily admission of fault or negligence, are the vital elements of such an enterprise. Such demonstration requires acceptance of the reality and acute analysis of the adverse outcome by the caregiver. Michael Woods'[1] *Healing Words: The Power of Apology in Medicine* summarizes matters via five R's: recognition, regret, responsibility, remedy, and remain engaged. Perhaps the most vital components of disclosure by physicians are (1) a clear explanation of the nature of the outcome and (2) a clear explanation of when results differ from what had been anticipated.

The Role of Apology

It may not always be apparent when an apology is appropriate, so recognizing fear, frustration, or anger may be the first sign that an apology should be considered. Keep in mind that an excuse should not be reserved solely for medical mishaps but is also appropriate for situations of less severity such as long waits before appointments, rude behavior by staff, or delays in returning telephone calls. Physicians who practice the Golden Rule and truly respect the dignity of their patients are sensitive to patient needs and can more easily recognize the need for an apology.

Expressing regret for the patient's situation, even when the case was not created by a medical error, shows a sense of compassion and understanding of the pain, anxiety, or fear the patient is experiencing. The responsibility then follows recognition. The physician takes responsibility for the patient care, disclosing the known facts and explaining that any unknowns will be investigated to prevent future occurrences. The last component of an apology requires an offer of restitution or remedy. The patient should be told what is being done to correct the problem, what the long-term effects will be, and who will pay for any additional costs.

Many malpractice insurers still take the position that admitting fault or apologizing to the patient will increase the likelihood of litigation and jeopardize their ability to defend the physician efficiently. There is no evidence to support the validity of that belief and, in fact, there is ample evidence to the contrary. In studies that have examined the reasons given for filing a lawsuit, patients and their families cited suspicion of a cover-up, lack of error acknowledgment, and failure to apologize as primary motivating factors. Many patients report feeling angry and frustrated because they were never given an explanation or an apology from any of their health care providers following a medical mishap. They perceived the physician's behavior as avoiding the issue or acting as if the complication or catastrophe was not a big deal. Studies overwhelmingly show that a policy of providing an authentic apology and full and transparent disclosure is the best risk management tool an insurer can utilize.

In my experience, involving patients and their family when unanticipated outcomes occur has been very productive. The physician should remember that the health care team includes the patient and their family; teamwork, another word for collaboration, should be present at all times, including after the discovery by the physician of an unanticipated outcome.

Policy for Disclosure of Medical Errors

In 2001, the Joint Commission for Accreditation of Healthcare Organization (JCAHO) required hospitals and health care organizations to disclose unanticipated outcomes of care or treatment to the patient and, when appropriate, to the family. We summarized some dos and don'ts in Table 8.1.

The standard states (RI.1.2.1)[2]: Patients and, when appropriate, their families are informed about outcomes of care, including unanticipated results.

This accompanying intent provision (RI.1.2.2)[3] indicates that the responsible licensed independent practitioner or his or her designee explain the outcome of any treatments or procedures to the patient, and when appropriate the family, whenever those findings differ significantly from the anticipated results.

These provisions had some controversy. The first step must be a collaborative effort between the healthcare team to develop a policy for complying with the requirement. Having a structured plan of action with pre-designated duties can help assure complete and timely disclosure of the event. The patient should be informed of the specific process and kept updated.

The following is a suggested outline of what disclosure should contain:

- An apology
- Simple explanation of how the event occurred
- Assessment of the harm
- Actions taken to treat the injury or address the problem
- Future preventative measures instituted

Table 8.1 Examples of Problems and Solutions in Approaching Patient

Patient follow-up	Misunderstanding	Written instructions
	Misunderstanding	Education in office
Medical error	Not disclosing	Disclose and discuss
	Afraid and distant	Apologetic and sincere
Patient plan	One-to-one	Bring nurse, bring family
	Focus on one issue	Focus on all issues to anticipate bad outcomes

- Responsibilities for ongoing care
- Supply a contact person for follow-up communications
- Offer of counseling and support
- Accommodation for associated costs

Section 8.6 of the American Medical Association's (AMA)[4] code of ethics stresses the need to disclose errors to patients:

> It is a fundamental ethical requirement that a physician should at all times deal honestly and openly with patients … Situations occasionally occur in which a patient suffers significant medical complications that may have resulted from the physician's mistake or judgment. In these circumstances, the physician is ethically required to inform the patient of all the facts necessary to ensure understanding of what has occurred … (Gailey, L. (2015). "I'm Sorry" as Evidence? Why the Federal Rules of Evidence Should Include a New Specialized Relevance Rule to Protect Physicians. *Defense Counsel Journal*, 82(2), 172.). Concern about legal liability, which might result from truthful disclosure, should not affect the physician's honesty with a patient.

By placing the patient's best interest above their own, physicians can offer a sincere apology and, when necessary, begin the healing process and ask the patients forgiveness.

Notes

1. Woods, M. 2007. *Healing Words: The Power of Apology in Medicine*. Oak Park, IL: Doctors in Touch.
2. JCAHO. 2001. Pain standards for 2001. Accessed at URL: https://www.jointcommission.org/assets/1/6/2001_Pain_Standards.pdf.
3. CRICO. Disclosure and apology: CRICO's perspective. Accessed at URL: http://www.mitsstools.org/uploads/3/7/7/6/3776466/disclosureaplogy_cricosperspective.pdf.
4. AMA. 2011. Code of medical ethics' opinions on patient safety. *Virtual Mentor*, 13(9): 626–628. Accessed at URL: https://journalofethics.ama-assn.org/article/ama-code-medical-ethics-opinions-patient-safety/2011-09.

Suggested Reading

1. Anderson R. E. 2004. Defending the practice of medicine. *Arch Intern Med*. 164(11): 1173–8.
2. Claim Trend Analysis. 2004. ed. Rockville, MD: Physician Insurers Association of America.

3. Donaldson, M. S., Corrigan, J. M. and Kohn, L. T. 2000. *To Err Is Human: Building a Safer Health System*, ed. Washington, DC: Institute of Medicine.
4. Gailey, L. 2015. "I'm sorry" as evidence? Why the federal rules of evidence should include a new specialized relevance rule to protect physicians. *Defense Counsel Journal* 82(2): 172–9.
5. Harming Patient Access to Care: The Impact of Excessive Litigation. 2002. In: *Subcommittee on Health Committee on Energy and Commerce*. Washington, DC, US Government Printing Office, 107–27.
6. Lucius Annaeus Seneca, *De Clementia* 1.9.1.1. (n. d.). Accessed at URL: http://latin.packhum.org/loc/1017/14/6#6.
7. Patient Rights Causes, Symptoms, Treatment - Emedicinehealth. (n.d.). Accessed at URL: https://www.emedicinehealth.com/patient_rights/page2_em.htm.
8. *Profitability by Line by State in 1976 and 2002*. 2003. ed. Kansas City, MO: National Association of Insurance Commissioners.
9. Ri-055 Disclosure Of Unanticipated Outcomes. Accessed at URL: http://www.sjo-magnet.org/documents/Organizational_Overview/OO14.3.
10. US Department of Health and Human Services. 2002. *Confronting the New Health Care Crisis: Improving Health Care Quality and Lowering Costs by Fixing Our Medical Liability System*, ed. Washington, DC: Office of the Assistant Secretary for Planning and Evaluation.

Ethics Summary Table

How to Disclose Errors

Error is part of human life.

Continually making errors is not acceptable.

Metrics are there to monitor the physician.

In case of confusion protocols should be followed.

Miscommunication needs to be avoided.

Use electronic medical system tools for avoiding communication errors.

Do not be afraid to admit errors.

An apology is still good ethical behavior.

Always involve patient and family in decisions and when disclosing errors.

Chapter 9

Consent and Conflict of Interest

There is a fear in our society toward the medical profession, and there is an erosion of the public's confidence in the profession.

When a physician acts in an unethical way it harms not only the individual patient but also the doctor–patient relationship and the relationship society has with doctors. Unethical behavior in the context of drug company-sponsored clinical trials multiplies the harm to society, affecting its relationship with the research enterprise and with the health care industry.

Consent

Consent was seen as a formality, a preamble to treatment. Nowadays informed consent is an essential part of the ethical practice of medicine. It represents the opportunity to solidify the doctor–patient relationship. Valid informed consent describes the shift in primary care medicine to guide rather than dictate an individual's health care decisions. This has been the road to the *shared decision making*. Furthermore, informed consent is increasingly relevant in today's evolving legislative expectations and health care initiatives.

The physician has direct control over the process of informed consent than any other areas of medicine and can explain in better detail the pros and cons of the treatment or surgery. It is time consuming but it is time well spent. Thus, incorporating improvements to the process of informed consent is time well invested.

What is an Informed Consent

Informed consent is a needed process in which the patient learns and understands the purpose, benefits, and potential risks of medical or surgical intervention.

Informed consent needs to include more details and alternative treatments and the possibilities of stopping medication in case they participate in a trial. The benefits of patient involvement in clinical trials and their alternatives to participation should be spelled out.

Informed consent is about patient's understanding and willingness to participate in any study and not about signing a form. Prospective participants in any research study must understand the purpose, the procedures, the potential risks and benefits.

By Joint Commission's interpretation, communication between a clinician and a patient that results in the patient's authorization or agreement to undergo a specific medical intervention (see sidebar box for The Joint Commission's glossary definition). In addition to the process of communicating with their patients, clinicians are concerned with obtaining the evidence of consent that serves to document their legal and ethical responsibility. Unfortunately, the emphasis on getting a patient's signature as documentation of informed consent results in different effectiveness of the communication between a clinician and a patient. Communication issues are the most frequent cause of serious adverse events reported to The Joint Commission's sentinel event database.[1]

Patient autonomy strives towards equality in this partnership, but a significant change in law and medicine will change the relationship. Therefore, first was the requirement for a simple consent for the treatment, specifically invasive procedure.

From an article of 2012, Daniel Hall and his coauthors[2] reinforced the concept by outlining the following:

1. The process of informed consent in which physicians disclosed details about a treatment did not emerge until the 1950s, when courts first required physicians to disclose information customarily disclosed by experienced clinicians (e.g., the reasonable physician standard).
2. It was not until 1975 that American courts articulated the reasonable person standard, which required that physicians disclose the information that a "reasonable person" would want to know in a similar situation.

They concluded that:

> Informed consent is further predicated on the patient's or surrogate's capacity to make decisions — not only should the decision maker understand the relevant information, he or she should also be able to appreciate the information's importance and use it to weigh treatment options in light of their values.[2]

The Moral Purpose of the Consent

Hall and his coauthors also commented on the moral purpose of the consent:

> The moral purpose of informed consent is somewhat more abstract and ideological, seeking to respect patient autonomy by ensuring that treatment is directed toward the ends desired and is chosen by the patient. In this context, informed consent is intended to shift the ethical paradigm for decision making away from physician-centered models to more patient-centered approaches. The ethics literature regarding informed consent also emphasizes that it is not an event, but a process that precedes the "signing" of the document and continues for as long as the choice remains relevant. Thus, the consent to undergo dialysis or continue with chemotherapy is continually re-evaluated (and may change). The consent form should not be confused with the consent process; the type merely documents that the process has occurred. Importantly, other parts of the patient record (e.g., clinic and operative notes) should corroborate details of the process.

The Role of the Physician

Physicians themselves should be taking the consent from the patients since it is their time to bond fully with their patients. A delegation of this critical task could be dangerous.

In discussing the matter with the patient, the physician should cover:

- The patient's diagnosis, if it is known
- The nature and purpose of the proposed treatment or procedure
- The benefits and the risks of that proposed treatment or procedure
- The alternatives to the proposed treatment or procedure
- Alternatives should be discussed regardless of their cost and regardless of whether they will likely be covered by the patient's health insurance
- The risks and benefits of alternative treatments or procedures
- The risks and benefits of not receiving or undergoing any treatment or procedure[3]

Physician Conflict of Interest

- Before the event of managed care, conflict of interest was not even taken into consideration.

- In fact, managed care physicians running a business were not required to maximize their profit to make a good living.
- Reimbursement was not the issue even for a businessman who could make a good living practicing medicine.
- Physicians starting out were often told to take care of the patient, and the business of the practice will take care of itself but today this is not the case.
- A stakeholder is not just the individual patient but both the health care industry and the health care institution.
- Pool of people in a different direction, but unless such interest affects the patient care then no conflict exists.
- The conflict between the physician's personal interests and the interests of the patient and the conflict that divides physician loyalty between two or more patients, or between the patient and the third party (e.g. physician takes care of friends or family member).
- The critical requirement of the physician is the nonmaleficence, do not harm, while beneficence means to be useful and obey the company policy act and the organization's purpose.
- The rule for the conduct of medical research and for the practice of medicine is truth-telling and full disclosure in analysis and in the clinical scenario; it admits of no exception and is binding.
- When someone purchases a car, no one expects full disclosure on the price. The buyer does not disclose how much they are willing to pay nor does the dealer disclose the least they are willing to accept.

Declaration of Helsinki

The Declaration of Helsinki after the World War II outlines the principle of independence and autonomy of patients by disallowed experiments and clinical trials on innocent or not informed subjects.

- Much of the attention in the press came from the clinical care investigation published in 1947 regarding the first medical milestone research and establishment of the perceptive ethical human analysis.
- The Medical Association released the Declaration of Helsinki in 1964. In 1974 a revision of the coalition recommended a review of protocol by an independent committee.
- The United States published additional information and guidelines on the policy.
- The policy called for review of oversights by an independent committee to ensure they were right and that the welfare of those involved and methods for obtaining consent described the purpose of the procedure.
- That is why institutional review boards were created.

Enrolling Patients in Studies

According to the National Institute of Health[4] (NIH), individuals should be treated with respect from the time they are approached for possible participation—even if they refuse enrollment in a study—throughout their involvement and after their participation ends. This includes:

■ Respecting their privacy and keeping their private information confidential.

■ Respecting their right to change their mind, to decide that the research does not match their interests, and to withdraw without penalty.

■ Informing them of new information that might emerge in the course of research, which might change their assessment of the risks and benefits of participating.

■ Monitoring their welfare and, if they experience adverse reactions, untoward events, or changes in clinical status, ensuring appropriate treatment and, when necessary, removal from the study.

■ Informing them about what was learned from the research. Most researchers do an excellent job of monitoring the volunteers' welfare and making sure they are okay. They are not always so good about distributing the study results. If they don't tell you, ask.

■ It is impossible to give an exhaustive list of situations that might present a conflict. However, among the most common situations that may constitute a conflict are: holding an interest in or accepting free or discounted goods from any company or organization that does, or is seeking to do, business with the institution by any employee who is in a position to directly or indirectly influence either the institution's decision to do business, or the terms upon which business would be done with such company or organization.

■ Holding an interest in a group that competes with the institution.

■ Being employed by (including working as a consultant) or serving on the board of any organization that does, or is seeking to do, business with the University or which competes with the institution.

■ Gaining personally, e.g., through commissions, loans, expense or travel reimbursements, or other compensation, from any company or organization doing, or seeking to do, business with the institution.[5]

Disclosure: Research and Financial Relationship with Business

A 1992 study published in *The New England Journal of Medicine*[6] found that doctors with investments in radiation sites prescribed such treatments more often than doctors without the direct financial interest. Physicians have been found to be susceptible to economic temptation. These relationships vary in the amount and method of compensation that a physician receives and in the amount of control the physician can exercise over the enterprise. The relationships promote patient welfare as well as providing the potential for a conflict of interest. Disclosure of funding sources, institutional affiliations, and potential conflicts of interest is necessary to overcome the perception of selfishness. Federal laws govern some of these relations and are essential for the physician to understand, e.g., stark, safe-harbor regulation and the nature of administrative law courts, and the Inspector General.

Disclosure does not always minimize the risks and harms to the patient. This is especially true when interests aside from the patients are not only present but driving the enterprise.

Disclosure to the patient does not relieve a physician, an institution, the government, or even society from the responsibility of being ethical. The ethical burden cannot be passed on to the patient, and the buyer beware approach is not an acceptable one. Disclosure only begins the process.

Objective criteria have been established to resolve specific situations in which a financial conflict of interest can be expected to exist (e.g., Canadian Association of Laboratory Pathologists, IRB and its guidelines based on the concepts of Respect, Justice, and Beneficence).

What Is the Future

Ethical standards need to evolve to keep pace with the changes in the environment. A combination of disclosure, legislation, adoption of policy statements specific to institutions, and professional associations combined with mandatory continuing education would minimize the risks to patients from financial conflicts of interest and begin to, once again, build up the public trust in the clinical care enterprise.

> The ethical pitfalls include financial issues such as patient welfare versus monetary gains, but also full disclosure and informed consent and possible consideration of motivation concerning stature within the profession as a surrogate of financial gain.

Notes

1. JCAHO. 2016. Informed consent: More than getting a signature. *Quick Safety*, 21: 1–3. Accesssed at URL: https://www.jointcommission.org/assets/1/23/Quick_Safety_Issue_Twenty-One_February_2016.pdf.
2. Hall, D. E., A. V. Prochazka, and A. S. Fink. 2012. Informed consent for clinical treatment *CMAJ*, 184(5): 533–40. Accessed at URL: http://www.cmaj.ca/content/184/5/533.

3. Findlaw. (n.d.) Understanding informed consent: A primer. Accesssed at URL: https://healthcare.findlaw.com/patient-rights/understanding-informed-consent-a-primer.html.
4. NIH Clinical Center. 2018. Ethics In clinical research. Accesssed at URL: https://clinicalcenter.nih.gov/recruit/ethics.html.
5. Fordham University. 2008. Conflict of interest policy statement. Accesssed at URL: https://secure.ethicspoint.com/domain/media/en/gui/22342/conflict.pdf.
6. Malloy, C. A. (n. d.). Informed Consent. Accesssed at URL: https://www.judiciary.senate.gov/imo/media/doc/03-15-16%20Malloy%20Testimony.

Suggested Reading

1. Frezza, E. E. 2006. *Medical Ethics in Surgery.* Woodbury, CT: Cine-Med.

Ethics Summary Table

How to Obtain Consent and Disclose Interest Conflict

Understand that consent is the essential part of treating a patient.

Consent is the time the patient gets to know you.

Describe treatment, action, and side effects (complications).

Use surrogate or alternative if necessary.

The nature and porpoise of the treatment only the physician knows.

Don't abdicate your vital role in making your treatment a team approach with your patient.

Disclose your conflict of interests.

Follow strict parameters to enroll patients in studies.

Ethics is overwise the standards of disclosure, legislation, and trust.

PATIENT
RELATIONSHIP

Chapter 10

Patient Welfare and Bill of Rights

Welfare

The fundamental of patient protection is based on altruism, trust, and competence.

The patient autonomy goal is to empower patients to make appropriate medical decisions by considering available notions and standards of care found from medical professionals or the Internet.

The medical profession goal should be centered on

- Patient welfare
- Medical professionalism
  The patient welfare is a multidimensional quality of the human organism corresponding to the degree to which that patient has realized the array of capabilities typical of the human kind.[1]

The World Health Organization (WHO) (re)defined health as "the complete state of physical, mental, and social well-being, and not merely the absence of pain and sorrow."[2]

Patient safety and health depend on prompt acknowledgment and reporting of errors in the clinical setting. Patient safety and welfare means that sometimes your "hands-on" learning will be shifted to a more observational or reflective mode.

Seeking medical care, places patients in a precarious condition. They place their lives in the hands of somebody else: a physician.

Physicians hold considerable power over the patient because they possess the unique knowledge and skill set needed to treat a disease. Years ago, this was left exclusively in the hands of physicians or nurses.

Patient Autonomy

The principle of patient autonomy is based on patient ability to be fully informed about the participation in all care decisions.

The commitment to patients' choices also led to a framework to ensure the patient's will is also available to make the decision even if the patient is impaired.

There has been increasing pressure from Medicare and Medicaid and the medical industry to provide tools to the health care system to provide better information to the patient.

The patient needs objective evidence and assurance that their physician is competent but also to ensure that the hospital is safe and produces acceptable outcomes.

There is an increase of patients seeking a second opinion.

Bill of Rights

Initially passed in 1997, the Patients' Bill of Rights was designed to increase the patient's confidence in the health care system. The Bill's aims were to build quality doctor–patient relationships and make the patients aware of their rights for proper care. It also obligates patients to take an active part in the management of their health.

While new features set out in the Affordable Care Act take effect, old rules in the Patient's Bill of Rights still apply. Beyond the fundamental belief in equality among patients, the Bill incorporates some other commonly accepted American attitudes.

The most important principles are listed below.[3]

- Health care should be available to everyone.
- Health care must be affordable.
- People who are particularly vulnerable deserve extra help.
- Health insurers should use their premiums to pay a reasonable portion of the cost of care.
- People should be encouraged to participate in clinical trials that result in new medications and better approaches to illnesses.
- Details of your health plan should be spelled out clearly and precisely.
- The patient should be able to quickly learn about the education, licensure, experience, and any adverse marks on the professional records of doctors and other health care providers.

- The physician must provide all the information you need to make decisions about your health care.
- No one else can make those decisions for you. If the patient is unable to make decisions (due to physical or mental health concerns), that responsibility has to be legally handed over to a designated family member or friend (health care proxy) or to a person assigned by a court.
- The patient should be able to acquire a variety of statistics on hospitals and clinics, including how often specific procedures have been performed there, comparisons between them and other institutions, and how to lodge complaints against them.

A patient's bill of rights is a list of guarantees for those receiving medical care. It may take the form of a law or a non-binding declaration. Typically a patient's bill of rights guarantees patients information, fair treatment, and autonomy over medical decisions, among other rights.[4]

According to the Association of American Physicians and Surgeons,[5] patients should have the following guarantees:

- To seek consultation with the physician(s) of their choice
- To contract with their physician(s) on mutually agreeable terms
- To be treated confidentially, with access to their records limited to those involved in their care or designated by the patient
- To use their resources to purchase the care of their choice
- To refuse medical treatment even if it is recommended by their physician(s)
- To be informed about their medical condition, the risks and benefits of treatment, and appropriate alternatives
- To refuse third-party interference in their medical care and to be confident that their actions in seeking or declining medical care will not result in third-party-imposed penalties for patients or physicians
- To receive full disclosure of their insurance plan in plain language, including:
  - *Contracts*: A copy of the agreement between the physician and health care plan, and between the patient or employer and the plan
  - *Incentives*: Whether participating physicians are offered financial incentives to reduce treatment or ration care
  - *Cost*: The full cost of the treatment plan, including copayments, coinsurance, and deductibles
  - *Coverage*: Benefits covered and excluded, including availability and location of 24-hour emergency care
  - *Qualifications*: A roster and requirements of participating physicians
  - *Approval Procedures*: Authorization procedures for services, whether doctors need approval of a committee or any other individual, and who decides what is medically necessary

- *Referrals*: Procedures for consulting a specialist, and who must authorize the reference[4]
- *Appeals*: Grievance procedures for claims or treatment denials
- *Gag Rule*: Whether physicians are subject to a gag rule, preventing criticism of the plan

Health Care Patient Plan

One of the most complex tasks for patients is to understand the health care plan. This is not a physician dependent activity but should be provided to the patient from their insurances.

The Bill of Rights has introduced a few rules about these procedures as well. These are:

1. Patients should be able to receive accurate, easy-to-understand information about health plans, health care professionals, and hospitals and clinics so that you can choose your care wisely.
2. That means that you should have the details of your health plan spelled out clearly and precisely.
3. All health plans must offer you a wide enough range of coverage options so that you don't have to wait for any services you need.
4. Women must have a choice of gynecological and obstetrical professionals, and anyone who requires the services of a specialist must be able to get them.
5. If plans do not fulfill these necessary provisions, you have the right to seek care outside of the program at no additional cost.
6. Furthermore, if you have a chronic or disabling condition and your health plan terminates your provider's contract, you may be able to continue seeing your provider for up to 90 days, unless the termination is for a cause. If you are in the second or third trimester of pregnancy, you may continue seeing your OB/GYN until the end of your postpartum care.[3]

Emergency Services and Discriminations

The Bill of Rights' outline also includes rules to follow during an emergency situation. It states: "You should not need permission ahead of time to use emergency services if you have symptoms that a 'prudent layperson'—meaning a reasonable person—would consider an emergency.

While this stipulation may seem somewhat unclear, it is meant to prevent people from using the convenience of emergency rooms rather than scheduling appointments in a doctor's office.

This right also protects patients by ensuring they aren't held back from using emergency services by health plans attempting to save money."

In the Bill of Rights, there is also room to define that everybody is equal and needs to be treated equally. Patients must be treated with respect and good manners, and may not be discriminated against for any reason, including:

- Gender
- Age
- Race
- Nationality
- Origin
- Religion
- Sexual orientation
- Disability

Confidentiality

Confidentiality is the basis of the Bill of Rights since everyone's health care belongs to the patient and not to anyone else. In the Bill of Rights, it is stressed that: "Healthcare professionals, insurers, and suppliers may not discuss your health history with employers or anyone else unless you permit them to, except if the exchange of information is necessary for your care, and in some cases where the law or public health are concerned. For more information on your rights to privacy, see the article in this series entitled HIPAA: Your Right to Health Care and Privacy."[3]

Right to Complain

The last significant point of the Bill of Rights is the "right" to complain.

The patient has the right to report and seek quick resolutions to any problems you have with your healthcare. Matters that might be of concern to you include billing, denied treatment, waiting times, how you have been treated, and lack of services.

"All health plans, providers, and related institutions should have internal systems in place to handle both complaints and appeals. The process for these should be easy to understand and participate in, and all rules should be made known to you."[3]

Notes

1. Koch, P.M. 2016. A theory of patient welfare. *UBIR*. Accessed from URL: https://ubir.buffalo.edu/xmlui/discover?

2. World Health Organization. 2018. Frequently Asked Questions. Accessed from URL: http://www.who.int/suggestions/faq/en/.
3. CMS. 2010. The patient Bill Of Rights: Your right to respect and good. Accessed from URL: https://www.cms.gov/CCIIO/Programs-and-Initiatives/Health-Insurance-Market-Reforms/Patients-Bill-of-Rights.html.
4. Wikipedia. 2012. Patients' Rights. Accessed from URL: https://en.wikipedia.org/wiki/U.S._Patients%27_Bill_of_Rights.
5. Association of American Physicians and Surgeons. 2018. Patient Bill of Rights. Accessed from URL: https://aapsonline.org/patient-bill-rights/.

Suggested Reading

1. Haack, S. 2014. The soul of medicine spiritual perspectives and clinical practice. *Ethics & Medicine* 30(1): 57–58.
2. National Active and retired federal Employee organization. 2017. When a Physician Drops Out of FEHB. Accessed from URL: https://www.narfe.org/index.cfm?fa=view OldArticle&id=4279.
3. United States Department of Health & Human Services. Accessed from URL: http://www.hhs.gov.

Ethics Summary Table

How to Protect Patient Welfare and Rights

Altruism.

Trust.

Competencies.

It is within the physician's power is to involve the patient.

Respect patient autonomy of understanding and sign of consent.

Everybody should have medical care even in a private insurance environment.

Physicians should provide care regardless of gender, race, and societal status.

Full disclosure should apply.

Patient should also receive easy to understand information from health insurances.

Details of treatment should be given by health insurances, hospitals, and physicians.

Health care organizations and hospitals are in charge of welfare as much as physicians.

Confidentiality should always be applied.

Chapter 11

Opioid Crisis

The Problems

The United States is in a period of an opioid overdose epidemic. Opioids (including prescription opioids, heroin, and fentanyl) killed more than 33,000 people in 2015 – more than any year on record. Nearly half of all opioid overdose deaths involve a prescription opiate.

Drug overdose deaths and opioid-involved deaths continue to increase in the United States. The majority of drug overdose deaths (more than six out of ten) involve an opioid. Since 1999, the number of overdose deaths involving opioids (including prescription opioids and heroin) quadrupled. During 15 years spam, 2000–15, more than half a million people died from drug overdoses. 91% of Americans die every day from an opioid overdose.[1]

We now know that overdoses from prescription opioids are a driving factor in the 15-year increase in opioid overdose deaths. The number of prescription opioids sold to pharmacies, hospitals, and doctors' offices nearly quadrupled from 1999 to 2010, yet there had not been an overall change in the amount of pain that Americans reported. Deaths from prescription opioids – drugs like oxycodone, hydrocodone, and methadone – have more than quadrupled since 1999.[2]

The most recent definitive data on the prevalence of the problem comes from the National Survey on Drug Abuse and Health, which surveyed 51,200 Americans in 2015. Based on weighted estimates, 92 million, or 37.8%, of American adults used prescription opioids the prior year (2014); 11.5 million, or 4.7%, misused them; and 1.9 million, or 0.8%, had a use disorder. The epidemic is spreading so rapidly that the numbers are likely higher now.[3]

More than 140 Americans die every day from an opioid overdose according to the Centers for Disease Control and Prevention.

In outlining its opioid plan, administration officials highlighted four areas. It allows expanded access to telemedicine services, giving doctors the ability to prescribe medications to treat addiction to those in remote locations. It speeds the hiring process for medical professionals working on opioids. And it allows funds in programs for dislocated workers and people with HIV/AIDS to be used to treat their addictions.

The commission of the Congress notes[4] that the committee had to mandate educational initiatives at medical and dental schools to tighten opioid prescribing, and funding a program to expand access to medications used to treat addictions.

The Congress is currently spending $500 million a year on addiction treatment programs, but that money runs out next year. The administration says it will work with Congress in the budgeting process to find new money to fund addiction treatment programs. A group of Democratic senators introduced a bill that would provide more than $45 billion for opioid abuse prevention, surveillance, and treatment. Not coincidentally, that is the same amount of money Republican sponsors included for preventing opioid abuse in bills that would have repealed the Affordable Care Act.

Another option from the Congress would be to restore a funding cut proposed for Substance Abuse and Mental Health Services Administration, the agency within the Department of Health and Human Services that oversees addiction treatment programs. In its 2018 budget, the Trump administration is proposing cutting the agency's budget by nearly $400 million.[4]

Classification of Pain

There are three primary sources of pain:

Physiological: Nociceptive and neuropathic
Etiologic: Malignant or nonmalignant
Temporal: Sopra tentorial

Why Patient Seek Medications

There are different reasons why patients seeks medication:

1. Runs out of medicine early
2. "Loses" medications
3. Requests specific medication
4. Claims "allergies"

5. Reports no relief with other treatments
6. Does not comply with other therapies
7. Refuses urine drug screens

The Chronic Pain Raising Problem

Opioid abuse rose dramatically between 1997 and 2007. There are few points to make on the increasing number of chronic pain:

1. The cost of chronic pain now exceeds the cost of cancer, diabetes, and heart disease combined, in the United States.
2. 50 million Americans suffer from chronic pain.
3. 70% are undertreated.
4. The United States, with approximately 5% of the world's population, consumes 99% of the world's hydrocodone.

Physicians are not ready since they often struggle with ethical issues in pain management. Therefore, the undertreatment of pain has increased as both a *public health* problem and a *human rights* issue.

Physicians have asked to be moral and legal gatekeepers in identifying legitimate pain patients. That started with medical school, since now the medical school curriculum rarely includes governmental regulation of pain management. For instance, 51% of Texas physicians believe prescribing long-acting opioids will lead to patient addiction.

From a survey done in 2011, Hambleton[5] reported:

1. The decrease in prescription drug abuse in children and young adults.
2. Only 19% of surveyed physicians received any medical school training in drug diversion and only 40% in substance use disorders (SUDs).
3. 43% do not ask about prescription drug abuse and diversion.
4. 33% do not obtain old records before prescribing controlled substances.
5. 66% of Texas family physicians are anxious about prescribing opioids for chronic pain.

Pain is the number one reason patients visit medical facilities. Various approaches have been tried to encourage patients and physicians to talk about and to allow for adequate treatment.

Every time a patient looks suspicious, they should be placed automatically in the database for control substance to prevent medicine shopping.

How we define a suspicious patient:

■ Complains about excessive pain compared to clinical findings
■ Takes more medication than is needed

■ Calls office for more prescriptions
■ Does not pay for their visit

We all, as physicians, should ring up the database to follow up on our patients. In Texas a new rule came out in August 2015: the New Rule 170.3,

> The physician must periodically review the patient's compliance with the prescribed treatment plan and reevaluate for any potential for substance abuse or diversion. In such a review, the physician *must consider reviewing* prescription data and history related to the patient, if any, contained in the *Prescription Drug Monitoring Program* and consider obtaining at a minimum a toxicology drug screen to determine the presence of drugs in a patient if any. If a physician determines that such steps are not necessary, the physician must document in the medical record his or her rationale for not completing such steps.[6]

The Role of Physician

Physicians are an essential part of the solution to the epidemic of drug overdoses.

Nowadays, patients can make a blog about their physician in any medical web pages. Unfortunately, only the patients that are unhappy heavily use the web to vent their frustration. Most of the time this is not legitimate.

A situation where just one unhappy patient makes a comment while the much larger percentage of happy patients do not brings down the online grade of the physician. This is an entirely unfair system for the physician, which does not indicate the depth of their practice and their knowledge. A politician will be happy if one out of 100 voters is against them, but a physician cannot afford that.

Therefore, most of the time the physician tends to give up and write a prescription for the aggressive and challenging patient requiring pain medication because they are the ones reporting the physician who left them in pain. Instead it should be the patient who is reported for abuse. The health care system is not set to help physicians defending against these abusive patients that can ruin their reputation. This increases doctors' stress.

If health care providers aren't well, it's hard for them to heal the people for whom they are caring. Stress and burnout among practicing physicians may play a role in the opioid epidemic.

As burnout increases, satisfaction with work–life balance drops. Many physicians feel like they are playing a never-ending game. They answer to a growing cadre of masters: faceless managed-care bureaucrats, managers, IT consultants, quality measurement gurus, and the problematic patient pretending they need more and more medications including opioid.

With the scarce resources and with the ethical duty to provide care for the patient including assuring that the patient has no pain and is excellent, the physician is then pushed into writing the prescription.

Given these pressures and demands coming from so many quarters, some adult primary care physicians may not possess enough time or the necessary emotional fortitude to explore non-opioid alternatives fully.

Possible Solutions

The underassessment of pain may be related to the physician's failure to assess pain often enough or correctly. Physicians are fearful of patient misuse of opioids and sometimes prescribe small doses of inappropriate drugs. Some physicians believe that a patient's increasing requests for pain medication always indicate a SUD instead of possible unrelieved pain or tolerance. Many regulatory agencies are involved in the use of controlled drugs, and physicians are fearful of disciplinary action.

The problem is that in particular states there is no DPS Database query. In other states, the pharmacy can double check for the name of the patient and the number of refills, and therefore, stop new prescriptions and the "patient shopping" with various physician to get more medication.

The Importance of the Database

Having a database that can be shared between pharmacies of different companies, hospitals, and doctors' offices is essential nowadays. Lots of patients in the past used "doctor shopping" to get more drugs from a different office. Therefore, the database will completely solve "doctor shopping."

The other things that this database can combat are situations in which a patient gets different medicines from different doctors and then creates their own medication in a homemade "cocktail." A database will bring evidence of "cocktailing." Therefore, we can eliminate the non-compliance, "do-it-yourselfers," prescription fraud. Unfortunately, when it comes to checking the database, the physician has to spend more time for no extra income. It should be a state business to cross-reference the patient so as not to further overwhelm the physician.

The Ethical Role of the Physician

The physician is to do the utmost to have a paper signed contract, mandatory urine for drug screens before prescribing further opioids, and patient referrals to a specialist if it gets out of hand.

The physician needs to keep a log of the patients to avoid over-prescribing. It is an ethical issue to understand the balance of treating the patient to their needs and abuse of treatment.

In the case of the opioid issue, the ethical issues are complicated to resolve. Physicians dedicate their lives to helping people; therefore, in the realm of chronic pain, there is always a fine line between treating the patient appropriately for their pain and overtreatment.

Unfortunately the physician has been left alone in this battle, and they receive criticism if they give medicine, but also, if they don't.

We, the physician, are the first line of defense for the opioid crisis, but also, the first to be attacked for the inadequate care of the patient.

Until strict rules are created to help physicians, we need to follow our ethical standards, such as:

- Provide compassionate care
- Obtain a pain contract or consent form
- Do urine drug screens
- Involve specialists
- Create a Prescriptive Authority Agreement with midlevel provider
- Don't look the other way
- Query the DPS database
- Document why it is okay to continue prescribing to this patient
- Require close to zero-tolerance
- Use pain specialists and psychiatrists

Therefore, all the physicians and health systems have to follow strict rules.

- Ensure one physician manages opioid prescriptions for chronic pain
- Limit refills to one pharmacy and develop a relationship with the pharmacist
- Give the patient the responsibility of making sure that medications do not run out on weekends
- Make provision for "lost" prescriptions
- Obtain consent for drug screens
- Obtain a release to talk to other health care providers and pharmacies
- Obtain a release to speak to law enforcement agencies
- Obtain signatures from therapists and fitness centers showing compliance with referral
- Document action taken for non-compliance with treatment agreement
- Discuss cause for termination from treatment
- Flag lots of early refills on opiates
- Issue red flags of drug seeking
- Discuss pain management agreement
- Chart extremely thoroughly

Notes

1. Paster, Z. 2017. Drug combos could pose a deadly threat. *Florida Times-Union*.
2. Fentanyl In New Jersey That Could Have Killed Millions Of. *Morning Star*. Accessed at URL: http://www.morningstar.com/news/globe-news-wire/GNW_7098677/fentanyl-in-new-jersey.
3. To Combat Opioid Epidemic, Be Honest About All Causes. Accessed at URL: http://www.commonwealthfund.org/publications/blog/2017/oct/combat-opioid-epidemic.
4. Allen, G. and Kelly, A. 2017. President Trump May Declare Opioid Epidemic. Accessed at URL: https://www.npr.org/2017/10/26/560083795/president-trumpmay-declare-opioid-epidemic.
5. Hambleton, S. 2016. Opioid addiction: The highs, the highways, the hopes. *2nd Annual Symposium on Addiction*. Lombard, IL.
6. Texas Administrative Code Title 22. Examining Boards Part. Accessed at URL: https://www.sos.state.tx.us/tac/index.shtml.

Suggested Reading

1. Alternative Medincine Foundation Information. 2006. An Alternative And Complementary Medicine Resource Guide. Accessed at URL: http://www.amfoundation.org/pain.htm.
2. Adelman, S. A. The Opioid Crisis and Physician Burnout: A Tale Of Two Epidemics. Accessed at URL: https://leanforward.hms.harvard.edu/2017/12/15/the-opioid-crisis-and-physician-burnout-a-tale-of-two-epidemics/.
3. Puzzle Tweaking: Tale Of A Wooden Stick. Accessed at URL: https://frictionalgames.blogspot.com/2010/09/puzzle-tweaking-tale-of-wooden-stick.html.

Ethics Summary Table

How to Fight The Opioid Crisis

- Watch for overdose prescriptions
- Watch for patient signs:
  - Runs out of medicine early
  - "Loses" medications
  - Requests specific medication
  - Claims "allergies"
  - Reports no relief with other treatments
  - Does not comply with other therapies
  - Refuses urine drug screens
- The physician should:
  Obtain a pain contract or consent form

Do urine drug screens
Involve specialists
Create a Prescriptive Authority Agreement with midlevel provider
Not look the other way
Query the DPS database

Chapter 12

Pathway for Difficult Patients

Types of Difficult Patients

It is quite tricky to define difficult patients. When the patient feels attacked, abandoned, or mistreated, they became emotionally unstable, and they can become difficult. In these cases that is a consequence of the treatment and of poor communication. Unfortunately, in many cases the patient can become difficult for a different reason. One of the most common causes is that they think they know best and sadly they have an infusion of culture from the Internet and maybe not from reliable webs pages!

Abandoned: Patients who feel deserted when you have run out of options. The best way to deal with them is to utilize second opinions, which bring a fresh perspective to the pictures.

Emotionally needy: Those are the ones who need more coddling than you have time for. In this case, consider psych referrals, both for help and for emphasis that we have more than a purely medical problem here.

Nobody called them back: This can be for the patients themselves or one of their relatives. It can be for different reasons, as seen below.

- About my mom in the nursing home
- About my pain after surgery
- About questions regarding my new diagnosis
- About my insurance company denying coverage for what I need
- Enquiring whether you have a phone version

Home problems: Some patients can have an adverse situation at home that they bring to the hospitals, and they cannot shake out. In this case, patient support personnel like advocacy experts will be highly suggested to be involved in the case.

Family problems: Families of patients can bring problems to the hospital and "place" the stress on the patient. Patient advocacy personnel could help tremendously in this situation even to understand if the family should be allowed to visit patient again.

Refusing Treatment

The American Medical Association (AMA) said that a physician should be able to deny treatment except in emergency situations. The doctors also have a choice in the ordinary moral condition.

Unfortunately, we are under continuous pressure, both the physician and the nurse, to provide behind medical care despite what the patient does.

Most professionals believe that this drastic step should be taken only as a last resort and as a means not to operate on any patient if it is anything but an emergency.

According to data from Wikipedia,[1] in the United States, the total number of stays discharged by the AMA increased 41% between 1997 and 2011. For adults aged betwwen 45–64 years, the percentage of AMA releases had risen from 27% in 1997 to 41% in 2011. By payer, the share of AMA discharges increased from 25% to 29% for Medicare and decreased from 21% to 16% for private insurance.

The available data suggest that, in general, patients discharged AMA have an increased risk of hospital readmission and potentially death. This information, however, describes groups of patients released AMA, and therefore, should not necessarily be applied to an individual patient wishing to leave AMA and who may have different clinical circumstances and risks.

This discussion, which includes disclosure of the risks, benefits, and alternatives to hospitalization, as well as the patient's understanding, should be documented in the patient's chart. While most practitioners believe that the AMA discharge form is needed to limit the liability, that is an invalid assumption and may, in fact, lead to coercive practices that do not support patients.

Some authors have begun to question the wisdom of this clinical practice of designating a discharge as AMA, as it doesn't follow professional standards, lacks evidence of its utility to improve patient care, and may harm patients by reducing their likelihood of following up.

Finally, there is a widespread ethical consensus that even when patients decline recommended treatment, health care professionals still have a duty to care for and support patients.

Accusatory Patients

The patient can be accusatory, particularly when there is a drug reaction. Therefore, it is important to include in the discussion the potential side effects of the medication.

The patient can be made aware about the procedure. It is essential to understand why they can be upset. It's important to realize that sometimes the family should not be included in the plan of treatment if the patient does not desire it since it would be seen as a violation of the Health Insurance Portability and Accountability Act (HIPAA).

At the time of a visit, there is consideration to waive the bill when there is a problem that is not valid when Medicaid and Medicare are involved. It's shown that the 2 billion dollars were waived, which was a significant loss for the health system.

The worst patient is the one who feels abandoned. They need to get a second opinion, they are emotional, and therefore, they need a psychiatric evaluation.

Most patients complained that when they called the doctor or nurse didn't answer the call. These patients need to be reported to risk management. Documentation is the best way to defend your treatment.

Watch out for all electronic gadgets since it is possible that *someone may be recording you*. Patients tend to use their cell phones to record and to take pictures.

Remember that some of patients are registering with the cell phone; there should be a policy of no cell phone in the office.

Consider a "no recording" agreement as part of the sign-in paperwork. The web is a great resource to find policies like in this case:[2] "We respect the strict confidentiality of the physician-patient relationship. We ask the same of you. By signing below, you agree that you will not make any recording of any person in this facility without their express written permission."

You should document all the phone conversations and the text messages to your office and back. A contract for opiates needs to be in place, and any red flags should be reported to the database.

Abusive Patients

First, we need to evaluate if:
- Patients under the influence of drugs and alcohol, or those experiencing psychiatric trauma, can be unpredictable and lash out verbally and physically at those trying to help them.

Then we need to make sure that this was not a reaction to:
- The shortage of ER nurses, increasingly crowded waiting rooms, and long waiting times can cause tempers to flare and people's patience to wear quite thin. Many nurses experience emotional and verbal abuse due to individuals

feeling as if their needs are not being met, or they are not taken seriously once they enter the hospital.

■ Patients are miserable and afraid when admitted to the hospital. Their insecurities, anxieties, and fears may surface in the form of verbal or physical abuse.

Verbal abuse and/or violence to you or to your staff needs to be reported. How do you terminate the relationship with the patient?

Try to resolve the complaint first and then transfer the care, which is always better than to terminate working with the patient, and make sure that all the documentation is in order.

A zero-tolerance policy against violence, aggression, and misbehavior toward staff or members of the public should be instituted.

Depending on the severity of the incident, patients may receive a warning letter regarding their behavior and be removed from the patient list.

A certified letter with a return request is needed, and the patient needs to have a plan of action for 30 days before the date of the termination of care.

Make sure the letter defines the goal clearly and the fact that they are not your patient anymore.

In your chart always summarize the advice you know the patient would not likely follow, e.g., stop smoking, weight loss, drink less alcohol, take a medication, etc.

Should the patient try to bring a lawsuit against you or a complaint to the board, the first thing to be consulted should be your chart. It is the most important the way defend yourself.

Physician Pathway for Abusive Patients

Most problematic patients do not to listen to their doctor. These patients can harm themselves as a result of this.

The patient who tries to prevent healing and the patient who refuses to treat a chronic condition can be considered a difficult patient. The most important part is that if they ignore the treatment, they should be informed enough about the risk that they can assess the consequences of not having the treatment. The physician must document that they decline the procedure. The best documentation will be a consent to refuse which is quite rare, therefore, the physician's own documentation needs to be available.

A problematic patient usually negotiates the antibiotic or other medication, particularly pain medication. Sometimes, the patient reports the physician because they don't give enough in medicine.

The physician is to do their best to have a signed paper contract and mandatory urine for drug screening before prescribing further opioids and refer to a specialist if it gets out of hand.

The physician needs to keep a log of patient visits. It is an ethical issue to understand the balance of treating the patient's needs and the abuse of treatment.

Physicians should follow pathways and procedures:

Get *somebody* to call the patient back and document it.

Get immediate help from a risk management or insurance company.

Validate the patient's feelings, not their version of the facts.

Actively consider billing issues and refunds.

Are Physicians Protected?

We should have more protection for ourselves. In this, I found myself in agreement with the blog of Ericka Adler.[3] She stated: "Dealing with abusive patients can be challenging for a medical practice. Although there was a 'Doctors' Bill of Rights Act of 1999,' which addressed a physician's rights about fraud investigation and enforcement by the government, no such formal 'Bill of Rights' appears to cover the rights of a physician about how he or she is treated by patients and others." She stated a few more important points:

1. Physicians have a right to be treated with respect as a professional.
2. Physicians have a right to practice medicine in the best interests of the individual patient and not in the best interests of an employer, insurance company, or another third party.
3. Physicians have a right to practice medicine in a way that best evidence and experience suggests, as opposed to being forced to make decisions based on cost containment, third-party interests, or the demands of patients for medications, treatments tests, or referrals.
4. Physicians have the right to expect that their services will be promptly reimbursed and that they will be paid fair market value for their services.
5. Physicians have a right to terminate a relationship with any patient who's abusive (including yelling or threatening physicians, staff, or others), who fails to follow directions, or who does not pay for/make arrangements to pay for services.

We all wished that there would be a substantial and complete bill of rights for the physician, mainly to take care of abusive patients, but unfortunately physicians are not protected adequately. The ANA came out with recommendations on how to deal with abusive patients.[4]

The rule is valid for everyone. There is no excuse for anyone to be rude, demeaning, demanding, or inappropriate to you even if they are sick. Health care providers deserve respect. And sometimes when people are rude, it is an unhealthy way of dealing with their situation. You need to command respect from them. There is no excuse or reason for them to treat you poorly. You do NOT deserve it.

Someone who is acting angry may merely be frightened, defensive, or resistant to what is going on around them. It is crucial for all of us to take a step back from the patient who is angry and ask themselves what is going on. If the patient is frightened, then you will have to approach them differently than if they are outraged over something, such as a long wait time. Even anger over a long wait time can mask a fear of not knowing what is wrong with them. The best course of action is to carefully interview the patient to draw out what they are feeling. Use reflective statements, such as "I can understand why you feel that way" and try to discuss possible solutions with them.[5]

Notes

1. Wikipedia. 2017. Against Medical Advice. Accessed at URL: https://en.wikipedia.org/wiki/Against_medical_advice.
2. Austin Primary Care Physicians. (n. d.). Office Policies. Accessed at URL: https://sa1s3.patientpop.com/assets/docs/17293.pdf.
3. Adlar, E. 2012. Abusive patient behavior: Physicians have "rights" too. *Physicians Practice*. Accessed at URL: http://www.physicianspractice.com/patient-dismissal/abusive-patient-behavior-physicians-have-rights-too.
4. ANA. 2016. How to Deal with Verbally Abusive Patients, August 19. Accessed at URL: http://www.americanrecruiters.com/2016/08/19/deal-verbally-abusive-patients/.
5. Lampert, L. 2016. How to Handle Difficult Patients. *Ausmed*. Accessed at URL: https://www.ausmed.com/articles/how-to-handle-difficult-patients/.

Ethics Summary Table

How to Deal with Difficult Patients

Give the benefit of the doubt.

Search for family or personal problems.

Give the potential to refuse the treatment and document it.

If the patient left AMA, it does eliminate the physician's responsibility if the departure is not recorded.

Make sure they do not feel abandoned.

An accusatory patient needs to be stopped and an ethics or risk committee needs to be involved.

Abusive patients are not allowed, and their behavior should be limited.

The best defense is documentation.

Physicians are not well protected.

The Bill of Rights for the physician is not recognized although it was created in 1999.

We have the right to terminate the relationship, but we cannot abandon the patient.

It is a very difficult situation for the physician.

Better structure for protection needs to be created and enforced.

Chapter 13

Non-Compliance and Patient Termination

Sign of Non-Compliance

Excellent communication skills, including active listening, are essential for proper patient care and compliant behavior. A provider's choice of words, body language, and even silence all play a role in how a patient receives the provider's information and advice.

Factors that can impact the relationship and give a heads up of non-compliance are reported by David McGrath:[1]

- Misunderstandings due to medical terminology
- Misunderstandings due to language, a hearing disability, or mental barriers
- Patient not realizing the seriousness of the condition or urgency of the situation
- Patient not having insurance coverage or money to pay for the recommended medications, tests, or treatment
- Patient believing the therapy will be embarrassing or uncomfortable
- Patient deciding to go elsewhere for treatment
- Patient simply forgetting

Ask Patient About Compliance

We can review visit frequency, missed appointments, and monitoring parameters. We can obtain other relevant information from patients as advised by Clardy and Visser[2] in the following:

1. Ask the patient to describe how s/he understands his or her medical disorder in his or her own words.
2. Ask if the patient understands the purpose of treatment and the consequences of ineffective therapy.
3. Have the patient explain the specific treatment recommendations you agree on in detail.
4. Using open-ended questions, ask if the patient feels confident in following the treatment recommendations.

The solution? If the patient sees any problems, we should work mutually to find answers with compliance.

Screen for the four D's:- denial, depression, dependence (alcohol and drug), and dementia.

Look for *cultural issues* that may affect care and ask if the *cost of treatment* is a problem.

Strain on the Relationship

The relation between physician and patient can be a significant strain when the patient feels let down by the instructional medication that the physician prescribes.

Who is a non-compliant patient? He/she is the one who does not follow the physician's instructions by:

1. Not taking medication
2. Not coming back for surgery
3. Refusing medication

The physician and/or the nurse is supposed to tell the patient what they expect from them, what the treatment is, and how the treatment is going to work. The patient must understand the treatment and follow up accordingly.

Most patients would not want to alienate their health care provider before an operation, therefore, most patients are compliant in preoperative situations and do whatever the surgeon suggests immediately after the surgery. It is only a while after the surgery that they start to be not compliant.

Non-adherence or non-compliance with prescribed medical regimens for a variety of disorders and diseases is a severe problem in pediatric, adult, and elderly population groups, both among males and females and among people of all ethnic, cultural, and religious backgrounds. Such poor compliance or non-compliance may have severely detrimental effects on the patient's health and quality of life and may lead to additional morbidity and mortality.

What Are Possible Physicians Strategies?

Strategies to combat patient non-compliance are well reported again by McGrath.[3] He suggested:

Educating patients regarding the recommended treatment or test and why it is necessary.

- Inform patients regarding any alternatives, benefits, risks, and complications associated with the proposed treatment or test.
- Provide clear oral and written instructions to patients, using interpreters as necessary.
- Emphasize the seriousness of the condition and the urgency of the recommended treatment or test.
- Schedule referral and follow-up appointments before the patient leaves.
- Place reminder calls to patients regarding upcoming appointments.
- Follow-up on failed appointments.
- Document all non-compliant behavior including no-shows, cancellations without reappointments, and failure to follow recommendations regarding treatment, diagnostic studies, referrals to specialists, medication use, etc.

It is reasonable to expect a patient to share responsibility for compliance with your follow-up recommendations. However, whether a patient is compliant or not, providers should document in the medical record their instructions and advice to the patient regarding treatment recommendations, referrals, and follow-up care.

Enlist Support

It is important to enlist the support system:

- The patient's family and friends
- Colleagues
- Case managers
- Behavioral support agents
- Outside agencies

What is the Best Approach?

Dealing with non-compliant patients can be very stressful. A potential approach has been suggested.[4]

A competent patient is entitled to make autonomous decisions about the management of their care that conflict with the views of their doctor; you may wish to consider the following:

Write to the patient, setting out your concerns and indicating that you would be happy to discuss matters further should they so desire.

Schedule a review and flag the notes so that there is a prompt to revisit matters at future consultations.

Discuss your concerns with your patient. Acknowledge their feelings without necessarily agreeing with what they are saying.

We need to obtain the same respect we give to the patient.

Whenever possible, try to allow the patient to tell you why they are acting as they are, giving them a chance for their fears and frustrations to be heard. Analyze and assess the reasons for their anger and use calm, reassuring logic to help them overcome their anxieties and address unanswered questions.

Physician–Patient Relationship Termination

The physician–patient relationship is grounded in the personal relationship which exists between the physician and the patient. When that relationship becomes untenable for either party, dissolution of the relationship may become necessary. The Texas Medical Association[5] issued a memo discussing the general legal and ethical issues related to the termination of the physician–patient relationship.

The ten leading points are the following:

1. Abandonment of a patient may result in civil liability for the physician.
2. Abandonment is usually defined as "the unilateral severance of the professional relationship without reasonable notice at a time when there is still the necessity of continuing medical attention."
3. Proof of actionable abandonment requires a showing that the physician failed to provide "an adequate medical attendant" and also failed to give adequate notice.
4. The plaintiff must prove that this breach of duty was the cause of his or her injuries or damages.
5. Proper documentation of the notice should afford the physician protection from possible civil liability.
6. In addition to orally advising the patient and documenting that advice in the chart, the physician should send a letter to the patient and return receipt

requested to ensure that the patient is aware of the physician's decision. A copy of the letter and the return receipt should be retained.

7. The law recognizes that the physician–patient relationship is different from the arm's length dealings between buyers and sellers of commercial products.

8. Physicians have a fiduciary or trust responsibility to act only in the best interests of their patients.

9. The physician is judged to have superior knowledge, must keep information about patient confidentiality, and must provide patients with relevant information and alternatives before asking them to consent to treatment.

10. There is a question of whether the patient, by leaving "against medical advice," intended to discharge their physician. The splitting of the hospital could have occurred due to facts unrelated to the physician–patient relationship or medical treatment. If this is the case, the patient should be asked about their intentions. Otherwise, if the physician–patient relationship has not been terminated by the acts of either party, there is still an obligation to the patient.

Firing a Patient

The Texas Medical Association has given us directions on how to "fire" a patient.[5]

The connection is not dependent on the fact of whether the patient pays the physician money for services rendered. If that were true, then no charity care provided to a person would result in the formation of a physician–patient relationship. The same is true for unpaid fees: failure to pay does not automatically terminate the relationship.

As a result, a physician should not deny an established patient an appointment or cancel an appointment because of an unpaid balance.

So long as the physician–patient relationship is established and not definitively terminated, a physician owes the patient the same duty of care. Otherwise, there is a danger of abandonment (or at least a successful liability claim based on delay in treatment).

Notes

1. David McGrath. 2013. Dealing with A Patient's Noncompliant Behavior, August 14. Seattle, WA. Accessed at URL: https://www.phyins.com/risk-management/taking-care/214/general/dealing-with-a-patient.

2. Clardy, C. & Visser, P Visser. 2013. How many times must a patient be told? *CCHF Conference*, Atlanta, GA.

3. David McGrath. 2013. Noncompliant Patients: Strategies For Providers. Accessed at URL: https://www.phyins.com/risk-management/taking-care/214/general/dealing-with-a-patient.

4. Dealing With Non-compliant Patients. Accessed at URL: https://www.medicalpro-tection.org/docs/default-source/pdfs/factsheet-pdfs/england -factsheet-pdfs/dealing-with-non-compliant-patients.pdf?sfvrsn=9.

5. The Texas Medical Association. (n. d.). Termination Of The Physician–Patient Relationship. Accessed at URL: https://tma.custhelp.com/ci/fattach/get/18682/0/filename/Physician+Patient+Termination.

Ethics Summary Table

How to Deal with Non-Compliance and Termination

Sign of non-compliance

Misunderstandings;

Language and hearing disability;

Mental barriers;

Understanding the seriousness of the condition;

Patient not having insurance coverage or money to pay for the recommended medications, tests, or treatments;

Patient believing the therapy will be embarrassing or uncomfortable;

Patient deciding to go elsewhere for treatment;

Patient simply forgetting.

Document encounters and problems every time.

Get a second opinion.

Involve the ethics committee.

Involve risk management.

Inform the patient of the alternative.

Be careful filling out documentation.

The hospital wants the patient to be happy and wants to avoid complaints.

The hospital will be not supportive of this situation as it will affect their public image.

You are alone.

RESOURCES ALLOCATIONS

Chapter 14

Pathway for Difficult Physician

Physician Conduct

In general, if you have a good sense of conduct and respect you have done more than 50% of the job. No cognitive test or scale can replace the following human attributes:

- Respect
- Good manners
- Applicability
- Ability to talk to different people in the same manner
- Controlling compulsion
- Controlling excess behavior

In general, what is expected from a physician's professional behavior? Here is what we came up with, which are requirements of the clinical profession:

- Good communication skills
- Patient advocate
- Good manners
- Good listener
- Good morals

Behavior indicative of misconduct is also easy to spot; you do not have to do too much. Here are some examples:

- Lack of respect
- Lack of dignity
- Lack of empathy
- Screaming
- Throwing materials
- Using offensive language

Those were obvious, but there are some that are subtler, which are still considered significant misconducts, such as:

- Not being responsive to nurse and colleagues
- Not being focused on the problems
- Emotional and not objective
- Poor chart keeping
- Raised voice
- Changed conduct
- Repeat offenses are defined as disruptive

Disruptive Behaviors

It is any conduct that disrupts and poses a threat to patient care. Such disruptive behavior may include, but is not limited to, an action such as:

1. Attacks – verbal or physical – leveled at physicians, patients, and staff.
2. Impertinent and inappropriate comments or written or verbal statements to patients and staff.
3. The nonconstructive criticism that is addressed to its recipient in such a way as to intimidate, undermine confidence, belittle, or imply stupidity or incompetence.
4. Refusal to accept hospital commitments made.
5. Sexual, racial, or other harassment.

Disruptive behaviors are well defined in hospital policies. Here, we would like to give some simple examples of behaviors which qualify as disruptive. Some of them are obvious; some are more indirect.

Obvious:

- Abusive language
- Physical contact
- Intimidation
- Sexual harassment
- Racial comments

Indirect:

- Bad communications affecting:
    - Colleagues
    - Nurses
    - Patients
    - Families
    - Bad judgments
    - Bad outcomes

Impaired Physician

The American Medical Association defines impairment as the inability "to practice medicine with reasonable skill and safety to patients because of a physical or mental illness, including deterioration through the aging process or loss of motor skill, or excessive use or abuse of drugs, including alcohol."[1]

What represents impairment?

1. A decline in physical or cognitive function due to medical or psychiatric illness or
2. Abuse of alcohol, illegal prescription or nonprescription drugs, or
3. Use or abuse of illicit drugs or other substances.

If any of these signs are present, a report should be filed within the administration and the Medical Executive Committee (MEC) should take action:

1. The statement must be factual and include a description of the incident(s) that led to the belief that the practitioner might be impaired.
2. Proof of impairment is not required.
3. A practitioner who thinks that s/he may have a disability may make a confidential self-report.
4. The confidentiality of the person reporting or the self-referred practitioner will be maintained except as limited by law, ethical obligation, or when the safety of a patient is threatened.

How to Approach Disruptive Behavior and Regain Professionalism?

The objective of the medical society and peers is to provide a mechanism for timely reporting and treating of disruptive conduct and to ensure quality patient care by promoting a safe, cooperative, and professional health care environment.

The goal is to protect patients, families, health care providers and colleagues from possible disruptive behavior and its consequences.

Documentation of Disruptive Behavior

Documentation of disruptive conduct is crucial as that will be the basis of all investigation and needs to be detailed in case of legal action.

Documentations should go to CMO, CEO, and MEC. Most hospitals have a Disruptive Practitioner Behavior Report Form (the "report"), which needs to be filled with details of the disruptive patient's name, dates of the incidences, people involved, circumstances, description of the factual data, and possible consequences.

Investigation and Corrections

The chief of staff, CMO, or the physician leader should interview employers and get the facts straight within 72 hours. Research should be within the peer review arena until some criminal issues are founded. The report should report the event and determined the action that is taken.

The incident should be discussed with the physician and a warning given.

Suggested Algorithm

As per working in the administration of a few hospitals and for some agencies, we came up with simple sequential action.

The first is what we call *AIDS*, which aims to help the rehabilitation of the physician:

- Approach
- Investigate
- Discuss
- Suggest
- Resolve

The second we called *ALERT*, which is along the same lines as *AIDS* but is an action by the health care system:

- Approach
- Investigate
- Define the problem
- Refer for evaluation
- Treatment

The system should not prove the physician guilty; until proven otherwise, it should give the physician the benefit of the doubt. A support system needs to be built for the physician of a circle of people – colleagues and coworkers they can use when in trouble. This will avoid burnout and suicide. The circle of support should be the following:

■ Colleagues
■ Mentoring
■ Counselor
■ Outside help
■ Find resources to help

The goal is to support the physician and to avoid possible avoidable sham peer reviews.

By sham we mean: A person or entity or medical peer review committee that participates in medical peer review activity or furnishes records, information, and assistance to peer review, without malice is immune from any civil liability arising from the act.[2]

It is important then to also have a measure of competencies in place if there is a competency issue that evolves into misbehavior.

Rehabilitation. The hospital and medical staff leadership shall assist the practitioner in their effort to find a rehabilitation program.

Reinstatement. Upon sufficient proof that a practitioner has completed a rehabilitation program, the hospital may consider reinstating the practitioner's privileges and medical staff membership. In reviewing an impaired practitioner for reinstatement, the hospital and medical staff leadership must consider that the care interests of patients are paramount.

Voluntary Disclosure. Practitioners who voluntarily admit to having substance abuse problems and request assistance. They will be allowed to take a leave of absence to seek evaluation and treatment. No disciplinary action will be taken.

Notes

1. The Impaired Physician (practitioner) Is One Who Is Unable. Accessed at URL: https://www.carolinashealthcare.org/documents/cmcnortheast/MedStaff_impairedMD%5.
2. State of New Jersey. 2016. Any Civil Liability Arising From the Act. S2040. Accessed at URL: http://www.njleg.state.nj.us/2016/Bills/S2500/2040_I1.HTM.

Suggested Reading

1. Gessler, R., A. Rosenstein, and L. Ferron. 2012. How to handle disruptive physician behaviors. *American Nurse Today*, 7 (11): 8–10.
2. Lim, M. 2003. Who is being difficult? Addressing the determinants of difficult patient–physician relationships. *Virtual Mentor* 5 (4).

3. Schwartz, S. K. 2012. Managing Difficult Medical Practice Employees Physician. Practice. Accessed at URL: http://www.physicianspractice.com/managers-administrators/managing-difficult-medical-practice-employees.
4. Towers, A. L. 2013. Clinical Documentation Improvement—A Physician Perspective: Insider Tips for getting Physician Participation in CDI Programs. Accessed at URL: http://library.ahima.org/doc?oid=106669#.WoXoK0xFw2w.

Ethics Summary Table

How to Deal with Difficult Physicians

State the problem clearly.
Have an informal meeting with the physician.
File unofficial report.
File official report.
Find a support system for the physician.
AIDS, rehabilitation of the physician:
Approach
Investigate
Discuss
Suggest
Resolve
ALERT, action by the health care system:
Approach
Investigate
Define the problem
Refer for evaluation
Treatment
Final report
Reevaluate for privileges

Chapter 15

Legal Environment

Concerns

Every physician is concerned to some degree about avoiding involvement in a medical malpractice lawsuit. Protecting the patient from harm is no doubt a primary concern at the foundation of every medical practice. Any model of medical professionalism should include a plan to reduce both risks by utilization of protocols based on accepted standards of medical training and development of skills for effective patient–physician communication. This type of model can help reduce the number of medical errors or unanticipated outcomes which occur and assist the physician in managing those events that cannot be efficiently avoided.

The legal aspect of the medical profession from physician to health care practitioner is concerned to some degree in avoiding involvement in a medical malpractice lawsuit. Protecting the patient from harm is no doubt a primary concern at the foundation of every medical practice.

Any professional should include a plan to reduce the risk by utilizing protocols and standard care, and it is best practice to develop skills for adequate patient care.

Almost every medical malpractice case stems from an unsatisfactory or unanticipated outcome, but only a small percentage leads to the courthouse. Why is it that some patients who suffer significant personal loss following a medical mishap never seek legal action? Effective communication by the physician is the answer. Communication that includes considerate care, frank disclosure, loving concern, and respect are the essential elements. Healing begins with the body and spirit and ends with the healing of the patient–physician relationship that was damaged in the process.

Interpreting the Law

Laws are not necessarily coercive or burdensome for doctors and other health professionals, but on the contrary, can be fine-tuned to try and reach their goal in the most efficient and least damageable way.[1]

Legal provisions may coerce physcians, for instance, if the law requires health professionals to report adverse events happening in the course of health care delivery.

The goal was to deter or even to prohibit professional behaviors that are deemed inappropriate. If the law is analyzed from the economic point of view, the damage is defined as an externality.

The central question is, therefore, to assess which legal rules can provide the best incentives to health professionals for delivering optimal care. In other words, the law must internalize the risk of damage.

In a law and economics perspective, however, to be efficient, legal rules should not give the incentive to avoid every possible accident that could occur, but only damage that could be avoided by investments in care of which the marginal costs are lower than or equal to the marginal benefits in accident reduction.

Oliver Guillod[1] pointed out that the law probably can have an impact on patient safety, even though the latter perhaps remains limited as long as the professional and institutional culture does not evolve. Combined efforts should, therefore, be made at the political, legal, educational, and institutional levels.

In the words of the Australian Commission on Safety and Quality in Health Care: "health service organizations should create an environment in which all staff are: encouraged and able to recognise and report adverse events; prepared through training and education to participate in open disclosure; supported through the public disclosure process."[2]

Laws promoting patient safety will have to strike a delicate balance between competing interests to create the right incentives while safeguarding the legal protection of patients.

The Patient Safety and Quality Act[3] (2005) states that:

The bill (Public Law 109–41), signed into law on July 29, 2005, was enacted in response to growing concern about patient safety in the United States and the Institute of Medicine's 1999 report, *To Err is Human: Building a Safer Health System*.[4]

The goal of the Act is to improve patient safety by encouraging voluntary and confidential reporting of events that adversely affect patients.

Malpractice

A key component of medical professionalism is the ability to offer a sincere apology following an adverse outcome that has had a profound life-altering effect. This excuse need not be an admission of fault or negligence but should be a demonstration of compassion and understanding. However, in some circumstances, taking responsibility for an error may be the best course for reestablishing trust. By taking responsibility and admitting mistakes, research shows that patients are almost 50% less likely to consider litigation when an apology and details of the error are disclosed. More likely than not, the truth will eventually be discovered, and non-disclosure of the failure by the physician will only lead to anger and feelings of betrayal.

Each year during the study period, 7.4% of all physicians had a malpractice claim, with 1.6% having a claim leading to a payment (i.e., 78% of all claims did not result in payments to claimants). The proportion of physicians facing a claim each year ranged from 19.1% in neurosurgery, 18.9% in thoracic–cardiovascular surgery, and 15.3% in general surgery to 5.2% in family medicine, 3.1% in pediatrics, and 2.6% in psychiatry.[5]

Poor communication has been established as a critical factor linked to medical liability claims. A closed claim analysis of 127 mothers who sued to cite perinatal injuries revealed that nearly all felt their physicians would not talk to them, answer their questions, or listen to them.

Risk managers, insurers, and malpractice attorneys all believe that the quality of the doctor–patient relationship is the key to whether a patient will sue his or her physician. Common courtesy, good telephone manners, and a pleasant office staff can actually decrease the frequency of lawsuits. Unfortunately, from personal experience, it is not true. I knew a patient, went out for lunch, visited his house: it did not matter! He still sued me at the first chance he got, and he was doing great!

In general it was found that the mean indemnity payment was $274,887, and the median was $111,749. Mean payments ranged from $117,832 for dermatology to $520,923 for pediatrics. It was estimated[5] that by the age of 65 years, 75% of physicians in low-risk specialties had faced a malpractice claim, as compared with 99% of physicians in high-risk specialties.

Honesty

If an adverse event occurs, taking time to explain what happened and answering the patient's questions honestly is imperative. The acknowledgment of an unexpected outcome or error, and an apology when appropriate, actually reduces the risk of a lawsuit.

A physician's ability to accept the reality that even good doctors sometimes make mistakes, coupled with a positive relationship built on effective communication can drastically reduce potential liability. The other extreme exists when a physician expects always to perform flawlessly, and therefore, finds it more accessible to place blame on others or to rationalize the situation. Making excuses and avoiding responsibility forces other providers to develop defensive attitudes and who, in turn, point fingers back at the treating physician. Stuck in the middle of this controversy is the innocent patient with no option except to visit an attorney to help uncover what they see as a pattern of deception.

Dr. Michael S. Woods suggests in his book, *Healing Words: The Power of an Apology in Medicine*,[6] that an apology has four key components: recognition, regret, responsibility, and remedy.

Manners of Disclosing

Patients do not understand science; they know manners. They look at your office and observe whether it is clean, if you look professional and have friendly, adept staff, if they have to wait too long for appointments, how long it will take to make the next meeting, etc.

Joint Commission on Accreditation of Healthcare Organization (JCAHO) required hospital and health care organization to disclose unanticipated outcomes of care or treatment. Even though JCAHO and thus the JCAHO standard has no direct authority over individual physicians, full disclosure is appropriate and necessary.

From a practical perspective, such disclosure is essential not only when medical mishaps occur, but also for far less severe problems, such as extremely long waits for an appointment, a lack of politeness by staff answering telephones, and, on the part of physicians, excessive delay in attending to nurse concerns.

Transparent disclosure has been shown by multiple studies to be a superb risk management tool; malpractice cases emerge from unanticipated outcomes, but only a small percent result of unexpected consequences produces malpractice cases.

HIPAA: Health Insurance Portability and Accountability Act

HIPAA became law in 1996, and its final compliance deadline occurred on April 21, 2005. HIPAA required the Department of Health and Human Services (DHHS) to develop and implement a standard for specific health information to protect the privacy of an individual's health data. Civil penalties for violations of this law have a maximum of $100 per violation and an overall limit of $25,000.

The goal of HIPAA is to limit disclosure of health information. Use or disclosure of an individual's protected health information is not permitted without permission of the individuals except as required by regulations. Additional state and federal privacy regulations exist and must be abided by, but none of these rules pre-empt HIPAA.

Persons who knowingly obtain or disclose private health information in violation of HIPAA are prosecuted under federal law with criminal fines of $50,000 and imprisonment of one year. In the instance of the criminal act being conducted by pretenses, these penalties can reach $100,000 and draw five years of imprisonment.

Transactions that fall within the jurisdiction of HIPAA guidelines are those that include an exchange of information that occurs in a national health care-regulated setting. While this general definition appears easily defined in its broadness, HIPAA rules are very complicated.

The information disclosure HIPAA guidelines, which can be viewed online at www.hhs.gov/ocr/hipaa, encompasses administrative, technical, and physical safeguards, all of which contain multiple standards and a combination of policies and procedures; moreover, the integration of all of the above together with privacy and security and electronic signatures are of utmost importance.

As a health care provider, every practice must take care to adhere to all HIPAA guidelines. This now includes the designation of a specific privacy officer on staff to keep the practice compliant continually; in some cases, and depending on practice size, it is worthwhile to enlist guidance from commercial firms who specialize in HIPAA-related consultation. It is also important to know that business contracts can be subjected to HIPAA law, and government guidelines are available at http:www.hhs.gov/ocr/hipaa/contractprov.html.

Notes

1. Guillod, O. 2013. Medical error disclosure and patient safety: Legal aspect. *J Public Health Res*, 2(3): 31.
2. McLennan S & Truog R. 2013. Apology laws and open disclosure. *Med J Aust*, 198: 411–412.
3. The Patient Safety and Quality Improvement Act of 2005. *AHRQ*. Accessed at URL: https://www.ahrq.gov/policymakers/psoact.html.
4. Kohn, L. T., et al., eds. 2000. *To Err is Human*. Washington, DC: National Academy Press.
5. Jena, B.A. et al. 2011. Malpractice risk according to physician specialty. *The New England Journal of Medicine*, 365(7): 629–636. Accessed at URL: https://www.rand.org/pubs/external_publications/EP201100158.html.
6. Woods, M. S. 2004. *Healing Words: The Power of Apology in Medicine*. Oak Park, IL: Doctors in Touch.

Suggested Reading

1. American Medical Association, E-8.12 Patient Information, Accessed at URL: www.ama-assn.org(updated June 1994).
2. American Society for Healthcare Risk Management (ASHRM). 2001. Perspective on Disclosure of Unanticipated Outcome Information. April, p. 6.
3. Anderson, R. E., ed. 2005. *Medical Malpractice: A Physician's Sourcebook*. Totowa, NJ: Humana Press.

4. Bernstein, A. H. 1987. *Avoiding Medical Malpractice.* Chicago, IL: Pluribus Press, Inc.
5. Kachalia, A., et al. 2003. Does full disclosure of medical errors affect malpractice liability? The jury is still out. *Joint Commission Journal on Quality and Safety,* 29(10): 503–11.

Ethics Summary Table

Recognize the Legal Environment

Be concerned about patients doubt and behavior
Good communications
Malpractice cases stem from unsatisfactory outcomes
Frank disclosure and disclosure regarding treatment
Law is coercive for doctors
Law is promoting safety
Bad outcome is a possibility
Apology is needed
Honesty from start to finish
Learn the manners of disclosing information
Be aware of HIPAA

Chapter 16

Electronic Medical System

Benefits

The electronic medical record (EMR) advantages include a single consolidated file for each person; capacity for data interfaces and alerts; improved interdisciplinary communication; and evidence-based decision support.

This is according to the National Institute of Health (NIH). However, ethical issues related to electronic health records (EHRs) occur when a patient's health data is shared or linked without the patients' knowledge; autonomy is jeopardized. The patient may conceal information due to a lack of confidence in the security of the system that has their data.

Security breaches and extraction of personal data are the nightmares of the EHR. Health Insurance Portability and Accountability Act (HIPAA) violation can be committed without even knowing the sources. If a hacker can infiltrate U.S. election and essential business companies, the EHR can be the next target.

The EMR has benefits in the nursing world, as reported by Christine Orlvosky,[1] where the industry may be slower than many others to replace paper records with electronic ones; the advantages of computerized systems are becoming more widely recognized. While the practice of employing EMRs in the hospital and other health care settings is still far from universal, the technology is the wave of the future. Even President George W. Bush called for all Americans to have an electronic medical record by 2010.

Also in the same article by Christina Orlovsky, she pointed out that "barriers, which include upgrading the technology of current systems and getting everyone on the same page, as well as the fact that there is no universal electronic health record system, but rather hundreds for hospitals to choose from, will only be overcome if a multidisciplinary team of health care professionals works together to make sure the systems meet everyone's needs. Nurses are critical components of the process all the way down the line. The key is for the nursing profession to realize all the benefits EMRs can offer to ease their jobs."

Handwriting Translation

The Msaddon blog[2] reported the following points.

One area EMRs help:

1. If the nurse is using electronic records, the physician is using them as well, and handwriting isn't the challenging element it is now with written records,
2. Another benefit of the electronic medical records is that it often works in conjunction with another valuable technology tool: electronic medication administration records, or eMARs, an electronic recording of time and date of medication administration, often tied to barcode technology.
3. When all the components are aligned, the nurse, patient, date, time, and dosage of medication is all documented in the electronic medical record.
4. Another nursing benefit of electronic medical records is the clinical component, which allows nurses to document clinical care. A nurse can enter a patient's health complaints, and the system can alert her to the patient's risk of falls or remind her to ask further questions about the patient's symptoms.
5. The ultimate goal of electronic medical records, according to Wise, is that a patient will be able to go to a new facility – either across the country or down the street from his primary care facility – and his records will travel electronically with him, allowing the health care provider instant access to his information.

Laura A. Stokowski[3] pointed out the following:

1. EHRs have distinct advantages over paper. The most recognized benefit is that the health care provider's orders are legible and clear.
2. Nurses no longer have to waste time consulting with one another, trying to decipher someone's poor handwriting, and fewer errors related to misinterpreted orders should follow. Nurses also like being able to find information about previous episodes of care (hospitalizations or visits) quickly and have all information about a patient integrated into a single place.

The areas that improved the most by introducing EHRs were:

■ Communications when patients were readmitted or received follow-up outpatient care;
■ Access to information can help the health care provider to make the correct patient care decisions;
■ The timeliness with which patient-related data are available; and
■ Legibility and clarity of patient care.

Computerized provider order entry (CPOE)

CPOE, implemented along with EHRs, is another feature that has the potential to improve clinician workflow, efficiency, and patient safety.

Unfortunately, some physicians still feel that the perceived disadvantages of EHRs overshadow these gains. These issues can be grouped into the following categories:

- Documentation time
- "Check-box charting"
- Point-of-care and real-time documentation
- Logistical and design issues

EMRs can add to work complexity by forcing better documentation of previously unrecorded data and because of poor design. Well-designed and well-implemented CPOE systems can streamline nurses' work. Generational differences in acceptance of and facility with EMRs can be addressed through open, healthy communication.

Physician Problems

We used to write and submit charges on paper; therefore, it seems that many physicians are resistant to make the change.

- It is essential when you start evaluating a medical records system that you have technical support from a person who understands IT. The next step is to find personnel, nursing staff, and physician staff who understand and can be your champion to evaluate the system.

It is essential to involve as many people as possible with meetings and pre-evaluation so that everyone knows when you will present the final product.

- Map your workflow using a flowchart or a modified flowchart. Workflow needs to be developed on paper. Deliver the chart to the software vendor selected for the practice so that the vendor will sell the program a flowchart that everyone is familiar with and approves.

It is essential to duplicate patient records and that we are capable of scanning patient records and information onto the system so that when the data is entered into the system, the system is updated, and everyone can access the same data at the beginning.

Setting up a training session is essential. This can be done either as video training, which is appreciated by many physicians, or it can be done by personal training.

- Use in-house personnel who make sure everyone understands what the problems are, particularly people who fear that, after we lose the paperwork, the computer could destroy all of the data.
- The process of learning is learning together with physicians and staff. Most people do not like to be imposed upon to learn a new system.
- Cut back on patient appointments in the beginning. This will give enough time for each physician to use the system without having the to rush from one room to another and concentrate on the data they input about the patient. This will not impact on the quality of care.
- Finding internal training is essential. I am sure that in an extensive system, the workforce can become a coach and leader of a system, and we need to find these coaches and leaders not just in physicians but in all of the other medical and technical components that will use the system.
- It is essential to find a physician who is well liked and savvy on the IT side who loves the project and who can influence others to get involved in the project.
- It is essential when you have new people who teach to give recognition to both sides.

It is of utmost importance after this is implemented to understand HIPAA privacy and security procedures. We need to make sure that the privacy and security procedures are in place when an EMR system is implemented.

How to Implement an Electronic Health Record System: A Five-Year Plan

One of the most challenging things today is to switch medical records from a paper to an EHR system. Many physicians are resistant to making this change. However, change is inevitable, and even the most resistant physicians should conclude that electronic records are most beneficial to the medical community and their patients. It is essential to understand that no one can implement the running of an EHR system in 24 hours; it needs to be done gradually, over some years.

First Things First

The first thing needed is to contact at least six to ten companies to evaluate their systems. You should ask for a request for a proposal and not just for a recommendation. The difference is that if you request a plan, including all of the new information about the system, the company will give you an economical rundown. It is too early to get stuck in the economic outline; you want to understand the system before proceeding further. You need time to evaluate the different medical records systems and to make sure that the system is compatible with any other systems in the hospital or practice.

The most important thing is that all of the parts of the laboratory, from the history and physical to radiology reports, can integrate with each other. If there is an EHR number in place, it needs to be entirely clear that the old data can communicate with the new data; otherwise, it will be a waste of time.

For most physicians, the purchase and implementation of an EHR system in their office will improve not only the efficiency of the practice but also its profitability.

Notes

1. Orlvosky, C. 2011. Endless nursing benefits of electronic medical records (EMR). *SCRN*. Accessed at URL: https://susiecookhc.wordpress.com/2011/04/25/endless-nursing-benefits-of-electronic-medical-records-emr/
2. Msaddon. 2012. The impact when caring and technology meets. Accessed at URL: http://msaddon.blogspot.com/2012/04/impact-when-caring-and-technology-meets.html.
3. Stokowski, L.A. 2013. Nurses speak up about electronic charting. *Comprehensive Cancer Settings*. Accessed at URL: http://www.ccsettings.com/blog-posts/electronic-nursing-documentation-charting-new-territory/.

Suggested Reading

1. Bill Siwicki. Accessed at URL: https://www.healthcareitnews.com/content/bill-siwicki.
2. Capterra Health. (n. d.). Electronic Medical Records (EMR) Software. Accessed at URL: https://www.capterra.com/electronic-medical-records-software/.
3. HealthIt.Gov. (n. d.). Health Information Technology Archive. Accessed at URL: https://healthit.ahrq.gov/key-topics/electronic-medical-record-systems.
4. HealthIt.Gov. 2018. Health IT and Health Information Exchange Basics. Accessed at URL: https://www.healthit.gov/providers-professionals/electronic-medical-records-emr.
5. HealthIt.Gov. 2018. What are the Advantages of Electronic Medical Records. Accessed at URL: https://www.healthit.gov/providers-professionals/faqs/what-are-advantages-electronic-health-records.
6. MicroMD. 2017. Advantages of Electronic Medical Records. Accessed at URL: https://www.micromd.com/emr/advantages/.
7. Practice Fusion. 2017. EHR vs. EMR, January 7. Accessed at URL: https://www.practicefusion.com/blog/ehr-vs-emr/.
8. USF Health. 2017. What is EMR? Accessed at URL: https://www.usfhealthonline.com/resources/key-concepts/what-are-electronic-medical-records-emr/.

Ethics Summary Table

How to Deal with Electronic Medical Records

Advantages include:

A single consolidated file for each person

Capacity for data interfaces and alerts

Improved interdisciplinary communication

Evidence-based decision support

Electronic medication administration records, or eMARs

Electronic recording of time and date of medication administration, often tied to barcode technology

Access to information can help the health care provider to make correct patient care decisions

Timeliness with which patient-related data are available

Legibility and clarity of patient care order

One of the most challenging things today is to switch medical records from paper to a EHR system as physicians are resistant to making this change.

Chapter 17

Telemedicine

Long Distance Consultation

Wikipedia describes telemedicine as telecommunication and information technologies that provide clinical health care at a distance. It helps eliminate distance barriers and can improve access to medical services that would often not be consistently available in distant rural communities.[1]

Telemedicine is the use of medical information exchanged from one site to another via electronic communications to improve a patient's clinical health status. Telemedicine includes a growing variety of applications and services using two-way video, email, smartphones, wireless tools, and other forms of telecommunication technology.[2]

Starting over 40 years ago with demonstrations of hospitals extending care to patients in remote areas, the use of telemedicine has spread rapidly and is now becoming integrated into the ongoing operations of hospitals, specialty departments, home health agencies, private physician offices as well as consumer's homes and workplaces.[3]

Products and services related to telemedicine are often part of a more significant investment by health care institutions in either information technology or the delivery of clinical care.

Even in the reimbursement fee structure, there is usually no distinction made between services provided on site and those offered through telemedicine, and often, no separate coding required for billing of remote services. Historically considered, telemedicine and telehealth can be interchangeable terms, encompassing a broad definition of remote health care.

Patient consultations via video conferencing, patient portals, remote monitoring of vital signs, continuing medical education, consumer-focused wireless applications, and nursing call centers, among others, are all considered part of telemedicine and telehealth.

When to Use It

Primary care and specialist referral services may involve primary care or allied health professionals providing consultations with a patient or a specialist assisting the primary care physician in rendering a diagnosis. This may include the use of live interactive video or the method of the store and forward transmission of diagnostic images, vital signs, and video clips along with patient data for later review.

Remote patient monitoring uses devices to remotely collect and send data to a home health agency or a remote diagnostic testing facility (RDTF) for interpretation. Such applications might include a specific vital sign, such as blood glucose or heart ECG or a variety of indicators for homebound patients. Such services can be used to supplement the use of visiting nurses.[4]

Who is Doing It?

Consumer medical and health information includes the use of the Internet and wireless devices for consumers to obtain specialized health information and online discussion groups to provide peer-to-peer support.

Medical education provides continuing medical education credits for health professionals and special medical education seminars for targeted groups in remote locations.[5]

How it is Delivered?

Networked programs link tertiary care hospitals and clinics with outlying clinics and community health centers in rural or suburban areas. The links may use dedicated high-speed lines or the Internet for telecommunication links between sites. The American Telemedicine Association (ATA) estimates the number of existing telemedicine networks in the United States at roughly 200, providing connectivity to over 3,000 locations.

Point-to-point connections. Private high-speed networks are used by hospitals and clinics that deliver services directly or outsource specialty services to independent medical service providers. Such outsourced services include radiology, stroke assessment, mental health, and intensive care services.

Long Distance Monitors

Monitoring center links are used for cardiac, pulmonary or fetal monitoring, home care, and related services that provide care to patients in the home. Often regular land-line or wireless connections are used to communicate directly with the patient and the center, although some systems use the Internet.

Web-based e-health patient service sites provide direct consumer outreach and services over the Internet. Under telemedicine, these include those sites that offer direct patient care.

The Benefit

Telemedicine has been increasing in popularity because it offers the fundamental benefits of improved access, cost efficiencies, improved quality, and meeting patient demand.

- *Improved Access* – For over 40 years, telemedicine has been used to bring health care services to patients in distant locations. Not only does telemedicine improve access to patients, but it also allows physicians and health facilities to expand their reach beyond their offices. Given the provider shortages through-out the world – in both rural and urban areas – telemedicine has the unique capacity to increase service to millions of new patients.
- *Cost Efficiencies* – Reducing or containing the cost of health care is one of the most important reasons for funding and adopting telehealth technologies. Telemedicine has been shown to reduce the cost of health care and increase efficiency through better management of chronic diseases, shared health pro-fessional staffing, cut travel times, and fewer or shorter hospital stays.[6]

Quality and Demands

According to the Department of Health and Human Services, about 16.4 million uninsured people have gained health care coverage under the Affordable Care Act. While this is excellent news for those who now have access to health care, it does put additional strain on health care. Telehealth software is one way to service more patients in less time and to reduce the overhead of patient check-in and waiting areas.[7]

The population of elderly and chronically ill patients is increasing. That's why 33 states have enacted telemedicine reimbursement parity laws and several others have legislation pending.

- *Improved Quality* – Studies have consistently shown that the quality of health care services delivered via telemedicine are as good those given in traditional in-person consultations. In some specialties, particularly in mental health and ICU care, telemedicine offers a superior product, with more essential outcomes and patient satisfaction.[8]
- *Patient Demand* – Consumers want telemedicine. The most significant impact of telemedicine is on the patient, their family, and their community. Using tele-medicine technologies reduces travel time and related stresses for the patient.

Over the past 15 years, study after study has documented patient satisfaction and support for telemedical services. Such services offer patients access to providers, as well as medical services, that might not be available otherwise without the need to travel long distances.[5]

Medicaid and Medicare

For purposes of Medicaid, telemedicine seeks to improve a patient's health by permitting two-way, real-time interactive communication between the patient and the physician or practitioner at the distant site. This electronic communication means the use of interactive telecommunications equipment that includes, at a minimum, audio and video equipment.

Telemedicine is viewed as a cost-effective alternative to the more traditional face-to-face way of providing medical care (e.g., face-to-face consultations or examinations between provider and patient) that states can choose to cover under Medicaid. This definition is modeled on Medicare's definition of telehealth services.[9] Note that the federal Medicaid statute does not recognize telemedicine as a distinct service.[10]

Medical Codes: States may select from a variety of Healthcare Common Procedure Coding System (HCPCS) codes (T1014 and Q3014), Current Procedural Terminology (CPT) codes and modifiers (GT, U1-UD) to identify, track, and reimburse for telemedicine services.

Ethics and Problems

If you google telemedicine today, a myriad of the companies offering physicians a chance to "boost" their income by doing telemedicine will appear.

This will represent an ethical issue for a physician and a more significant responsibility given the fact that "the art of medicine" included seeing the patient's expression and a personal exam, which will not be the same with telemedicine.

The rapid evolution of health care systems has significantly altered the roles and responsibilities of team leaders and how medicine is delivered.

In certain hospitals, either to contain the cost or for lack of specialties, telemedicine has become the primary venue to deliver medicine.

Nurses are mostly involved in order to monitor patients and to pass information to the long-distance physician. Patients have to adapt to see a doctor through the monitor.

In our experience, I saw telemedicine working well in the burn unit where the physician could judge from a distance if a patient needed to be transferred to the burn unit and can follow up with them in a telemedicine clinic.

Neurologists are now using more and more telemedicine, since there is a lack of specialties in many hospitals.

Critical Care is also using more telemedicine. I know a group from New York city providing telemedical critical care in an ICU setting in Florida.

According to the American Medical Association (AMA): "All physicians who participate in telehealth/*telemedicine* have an *ethical* responsibility to uphold fundamental fiduciary obligations by disclosing any financial or other interests the physician has in the telehealth/*telemedicine* application or service and taking steps to manage or eliminate conflicts of interests."

Physician Ethics Issues

The physician needs to have a license in the state where they give telemedicine consultation, medical malpractice, etc.

Team leaders are responsible for promoting safe and effective patient care and maintaining high clinical standards in all settings.[11]

Case law in recent medical malpractice actions has also affirmed the central role of the telemedicine doctor and the proxy in situ to prevent adverse patient outcomes.

The professional accountability and legal liability of team leaders in the telemedicine setting are examined. Practical strategies for reducing legal risk also are presented.

The physicians need to (from the AMA standards):

- Inform users
- Arrange a follow-up
- Be proficient in interacting with patients and surrogates electronically
- Recognize the limitations of the technologies
- Establish the patient's identity
- Evaluate the indication and safety of any prescription
- Document the clinical evaluation and prescription
- Inform patient about the limitations of these technologies
- Implement clinical and technical standards
- Routinely monitor the telemedicine standards

Using words from Dr. Shivan Metha:

> We should think about the same ethical issues with telemedicine that we have always considered in caring for our patients. If we focus on maintaining a strong patient-doctor relationship, protecting patient privacy, promoting equity in access and treatment, and seeking the best possible outcomes, telemedicine can enhance medical practice and patient care in ways that we can all feel comfortable with.[12]

Notes

1. Sheridan Benefits. 2017. Telemedicine. Accessed at URL.: https://www.sheridanbenefits.com/products-services/telemedicine.
2. Mdstaffers. 2018. Telemedicine. Accessed at URL: http://mdstaffers.com/services-2/telemedicine.
3. Campbell, J. 2016. Influences of Health Care Research: Telemedicine. University of Phoenix Online Class. Accessed at URL: https://www.coursehero.com/file/14807000/Influences-of-Health-Care-Research-Tele.
4. Siu School of Medicine. 2018. About Telehealth. Accessed at URL: https://www.siumed.edu/telehealth/about-telehealth.html.
5. Kaplan Univeristy. (n. d.).Why Telehealth Nursing?. Accessed at URL: https://www.kaplanuniversity.edu/news-resources/telehealth-nursing/.
6. American Telemedicine Association Telehealth Benefits. Telemedicine. *Ata Main*. Accessed at URL: http://www.americantelemed.org/main/about/about-telemedicine/telemedicinebenefit.
7. Chiron Health. 2017. Telemedicine Platform. Accessed at URL: https://chironhealth.com/telemedicine-software/.
8. Elite Health. 2015. Understanding the importance of telemedicine in improving health care delivery. *Elite University*. Accessed at URL: http://university.elitehealth.com/understanding-the-importance-of-telemedicine-in-improving-health-care-delivery/.
9. GPO. 42 CFR. Accessed at URL: https://www.gpo.gov/fdsys/pkg/CFR-2011-title42-vol2/pdf/CFR-2011-title42-vol2-sec410-78.pdf.
10. Medicaid.gov. (n. d.). Telemedicine | Medicaid.gov. Accessed at URL: https://www.medicaid.gov/medicaid/benefits/telemed/index.html.
11. Mahlmeister, L. 2006. Professional accountability and legal liability for the team leader and charge nurse. *Journal of Obstetric, Gynecologic, & Neonatal Nursing*, 28(3): 300–309.
12. Mehta, S. J. 2014. Telemedicine's potential ethical pitfalls. *AMA Journal of Ethics*, 16(12): 1014–17. Accessed at URL: http://journalofethics.ama-assn.org/2014/12/msoc1-1412.html.

Suggested Reading

1. 4doc.com. (n. d.). Welcome To 4doc.com. Telemedicine Made Simple. Accessed at URL: http://4doc.com/index.htm.
2. *AMA Adopts Telemedicine Policy to Improve Access to Care for Patients* [news release]. Chicago, IL: American Medical Association; June 11, 2014. http://www.ama-assn.org/ama/pub/news/news/2014/2014-06-11-policy-coverage-reimbursement-for-telemedicine.page.
3. American Telemedicine Association. What is telemedicine? Accessed at URL: https://www.healthit.gov/topic/health-it-initiatives/telemedicine-and-telehealth.
4. Asch, D. A., R. W. Muller, and K. G. Volpp. 2012. Automated hovering in health care—watching over the 5000 hours. *N Engl J Med*, 367 (1): 1–3.
5. Ekeland, A. G., A. Bowes, and S. Flottorp. 2010. Effectiveness of telemedicine: a systematic review of reviews. *Int J Medical Informatics*, 79 (11): 736–71.

6. Pew Research Center. Pew Research Internet Project. Health fact sheet. Accessed at URL: http://www.pewtrusts.org/en/research-and-analysis/blogs/stateline/2015/10/27/is-telemedicine-virtually-identical-to-the-examination-room.
7. Poissant, L., Pereira, J., Tamblyn, R., and Kawasumi, Y. 2005. The impact of electronic health records on time efficiency. *Journal of the American Medical Informatics Association* 12(5): 505–16. Accessed at URL: https://academic.oup.com/jamia/article/12/5/505/684713/The-Impact-of-Electronic-.
8. Smith, R. 1996. What clinical information do doctors need? *BMJ*, 313 (7064): 1062–68.
9. Victory Medical Solutions. 2016. Telehealth & Telemedicine. Accessed at URL: https://vmshh.com/services/telemedicine/.
10. Yarnall, K. S., K. I. Pollak, T. Østbye, K. M. Krause, and J. L. Michener. 2003. Primary care: Is there enough time for prevention? *Am J Public Health*, 93(4): 635–41.

Ethics Summary Table

Traits of Telemedicine

Eliminate distance barriers

Improve access to medical services

Available in distant rural communities

Medical information exchanged via electronic communications

Improve a patient's clinical health status

Primary care and specialist referral services

LIVE interactive video visit

Remote patient monitoring, including home telehealth

Need more medical education to provide this new service

Physicians need to have a license in the state where they give telemedicine consultations.

PHYSICIAN WELLNESS AND MORAL DISTRESS

Chapter 18

Balanced Life

Healthy Life

Finding a balanced life within health care has never had the importance that it has today. For many years, long hours, no resident work hours, constant availability, and no breaks were the norm. With the loss of the control of health care from the physician and overall with the crash in salary (from $3,000 to $350 for a cholecystectomy), the physician has been prioritizing the quality of their own life.

Every health care organization has always focused on medical quality and quality of care rendered to the patients. Very few, if any, were interested in focusing on the life quality of the physicians.

Most physicians felt abandoned and not recognized, not fulfilled, and not engaged.

There was a mild but significant negative correlation between burnout and engagement, and a weak negative correlation between compassion, fatigue, and satisfaction. Only intrinsic human factors were significantly correlated to exhaustion, work engagement, compassion fatigue, and joy. Medical society preliminary findings suggest that specific essential elements increase work engagement and compassion satisfaction among doctors.

The Change of the Pendulum

Stress and burnout will affect the physician's ability to take good care of the patient. Nowadays, many physicians perceive good quality-of-life as impossible.

Given, the temporary lack of comfortable situation, they look forward to retiring early on the job.

The most significant negative impact on the hospital is that if a physician does not have an excellent quality-of-life, they leave the hospital looking for a work–life balance and better control over their schedule and hours. They all now look for career satisfaction according to gender and age, which are soon found to be independent predictors.

With no surprise, the number of hours worked per week is directly correlated with stress, gender, money, race, and ethnicity.

Many studies show that more work hours per week were associated with increased stress levels among physicians.

Patient satisfaction has also been impacted by the stressed situations in which physicians have been placed. On the other side, job dissatisfaction has been the reason for physicians leaving their job, closing their practices.

As we all notice, the increase of hospitalist, surgical, and locum physicians are directly correlated with the search for a balanced life. Having an independent practice is not more financially savvy. Working for the hospital is becoming more stressful since the hospital is owned by a large corporation, and the contract is made in the "corporate style." The physician feels like a secretary hired to do a job for some hours a week but with much heavier responsibilities.

Most of the corporative contracts are made based on 40 hours per week and with much heavier responsibilities, but physicians are working possibly double those hours, and they only get paid for half of their working hours. Therefore, working a shift, like a hospitalist, or by hours like a locum, is a way for the physician to regain independence and be rewarded for the hours actually worked.

Going home without a beeper after their shift has been one of the most significant changes in physician's quality of life in most of the specialties. At the end of the day, there can be no hospitals without physicians.

Quality of Work Life (QWL)

The quality of work life is a quality measure adopted to balance stress levels at work. The QWL as a strategy of Human Resource Management has assumed increasing interest and importance. Many other terms have come to be used interchangeably with QWL such as "humanizations of work," "quality of working life," "industrial democracy," and "participative work."[1]

QWL refers to the favorableness or unavoidableness of a job environment for the people working in an organization. The period of scientific management which focused solely on specialization and efficiency has undergone a revolutionary change. Health problems interfered negatively in all domains of quality and were shown to have a relationship with labor activity. Driving or operating a vehicle, contrary to health care jobs, had a positive influence in the environment domain.

It was found that individuals who worked at night had higher scores for depression. Their scores were close to those found in individuals with chronic diseases.

This can lower the quality of care and increase the necessity for psychological responsibility for their health. Health services should prioritize promotional and preventive measures for quality of life of their workers.

According to the American Society of Training and Development, QWL is a process of work organizations which enable its members at all levels to actively participate in shaping the organization's environment, methods, and outcomes. This value-based process is aimed toward meeting the twin goals of the enhanced effectiveness of organizations and improved quality of life at work for employees.[2]

Hackman and Oldham[3] drew attention to what they described as psychological growth needs as relevant to the consideration of quality of working life. Several such needs were identified:

- Skill variety
- Task identity
- Task significance
- Autonomy
- Feedback

Warr and colleagues,[4] measured some work attitudes and aspects of psychological well being in an investigation of quality of working life, considered a range of apparently relevant factors, including :

- Work involvement
- Intrinsic job motivation
- Higher order need strength
- Perceived inherent job characteristics
- Job satisfaction
- Life satisfaction
- Happiness
- Self-rated anxiety

Quality of Life Scale

Analysis of the Work-Related Quality of Life scale (WRQoL) provides support for the psychometric structure of this instrument.[5]

The WRQoL measure uses six core factors to explain most of the variation in an individual's quality of working life: job and career satisfaction, working conditions, general well-being, home–work interface, stress at work, and control at work.[6]

Other issues influencing QWL includes a relationship with co-workers, professional development opportunities, and the work environment.

Potential sources of dissatisfaction with management practices include lack of participation in decisions made, lack of recognition for their accomplishments, and lack of respect by the upper management.

Not many studies are available for physicians but few findings regarding co-workers and the QWL are inconsistent. While some studies found nurses to be satisfied with their co-workers, including physicians, others stated the opposite.

In the nurse's literature, previous studies of QWL identified differing numbers of factors that have an impact on the QWL of nurses.[7]

One such element was the lack of work–life balance. In some recent research studies among nurses in the United States, Iran, and Taiwan, rotating schedules were found to affect their lives negatively, so they were unable to balance work with family needs. Additionally, nurses thought on-site child care and daycare for the elderly were necessary for their QWL.

The nature of nursing work was another factor that affects the QWL of nurses. The results of existing studies on the QWL of nurses indicated dissatisfaction of nurses regarding massive workload, inadequate staffing, lack of autonomy to make patient care decisions, and performing non-nursing tasks.

Childcare facilities, support for nurses who have elderly parents, convenient working hours, and sufficient vacations should be made available for nurses. These advantages help nurses to balance work with their family requirements.

Notes

1. Chand, S. (n.d.). Quality of work life: it's meaning and definition. Accessed at URL: http://www.yourarticlelibrary.com/employee-management/quality-of-work-life-its-meaning-and-definition-employee-management/26112.
2. Osboei, F.K. The relationship between spiritual leadership and quality of work life among employees. *International Journal of Humanities and Cultural Studies.* 3(1): 1848–1857. Accessed at URL: https://www.ijhcs.com/index.php/ijhcs/article/viewFile/1938/1701.
3. Hackman, J.R. & Oldham, G.R. 1974. *The Diagnostic Job Survey.* New Haven, CT: Yale University Press.
4. Warr et al. 1979. Scales for the measurement of some work attitudes and aspects of psychological well-being. *Journal of Occupational Psychology*, 52(2): 129–148.
5. Van Laar, D. The Work-Related Quality of Life scale for healthcare workers. *Journal of Advanced Nursing*, 60(3): 325–333.
6. Easton, S. & Vann Laar, D. 2018. *User Manual for the Work-Related Quality of Life (WRQoL) Scale: A Measure of Quality of Working Life.* (2nd ed.) University of Portsmouth.
7. Battu, N. & Chakravarthy, G.K. 2014. Quality of work life of nurses and paramedical staff in hospitals. *International Journal of Business and Administration Research Review*, 2(4): 200–207.

Suggested Reading

1. Aymes, S. 2017. Work–Life Balance for Physicians: the What, the Why, and the How, July 26. Accessed at URL: https://www.medicalnewstoday.com/articles/318087.php.
2. Bush, J. 2001. Life balance: 17 tips from doctors, for doctors. *Fam Pract Manag*, 8 (6): 60. https://www.aafp.org/fpm/2001/0600/p60.html.
3. Drummond, D. (n. d.). Work Life Balance for Doctors – The Power of a Positive "No." Accessed at URL: https://www.thehappymd.com/blog/bid/290781/work-life-balance-for-doctors-three-steps-to-saying-no-with-grace-and-power.
4. Martin, K. L. 2017. Is Work–Life Balance a Reality for Physicians? May 25. Accessed at URL: http://medicaleconomics.modernmedicine.com/medical-economics/news/work-life-balance-reality-physicians.

Ethics Summary Table

How to Have a Balanced Life

Focus on your needs.

Find ways to decrease the stress (travel, read, etc.).

If you feel abandoned, react.

Be part of your hospital physician team and support each other.

If the job is not right, talk to the administration.

If nothing changes, change position.

Focus on quality of work life.

Change hours in office.

Change rounds patterns.

Change or lighten up the surgical schedule.

Be involved in practice and hospital decisions that can affect you and colleagues.

Go to CME meeting and share your story with others.

Chapter 19

Spirituality and Wellness

Spirituality Models

Up to the last century, the doctor was the spiritual carer of the village. Most of the time the people that administered religion also governed medicine. Scientific discovery promoted the detachment between religion and medicine. Lately, there is an attempt to reintegrate this issue. As we probably know, in eastern countries, there is a connection between the spirituality and the body and the mind of a person.

The Zen is considered an integrated important issue that can help in healing and help in the well-being of the patient and the non-patient in their regular life. Improved health profiles can reduce health care utilization and enhance psychosocial function. It can improve the whole aspect of the patient.

The biophysical, social, and spiritual model reveals that it is divided into four steps.

1. *Biological.* Genetic and pathophysiological mechanisms are explained in this area.
2. *Psychological.* Develop and experiment different factors within the mind of the person.
3. *Social.* Culture and environment influences.
4. *Spiritual.* Assessment of individual spirituality and religion resources of each patient can help in the care of the patient itself.

Altogether, we need to find a peaceful balance between meditation, health care, the concept of spirituality, lifestyle, recreation, energy, fitness, etc.

Faith

Faith is regarded as a primary human force. A lot of people believe in something, and if it is not God, they believe in something else, but they still have a firm belief. A firm feeling in something non-tangible or a potentially unproved feeling which most of the time is described as faith.

Faith is something personal, something that you can change or improve. When patients are in need, faith comes stronger and sometimes can improve health profile, may reduce health care utilization, and sometimes makes them better. It could also have a negative impact if the patient thinks they are punished by the faith of the God that they believe.

It has been shown that there is a connection between medicine and religion. The people in the tribes that were administered medication were the religious power of the tribe themselves.

But there is also a large group of people that are atheists or agnostic who do not believe or think that religion is essential.

As a physician, we need to respect them all. We also need to understand that the social situation can impact the spirituality and the beliefs of the patient because culture or environmental influences are quite remarkable in their religious preference.

Assessment of the religion, resources, and preference is also critical when talking to the patient. It has been shown in the past that most people claim that religion is essential in their life and therefore a lot of patients will welcome a physician inquiring about their spirituality.

Others prefer no spiritual source or prefer not even to talk about it. Others prefer a non-approach with a nonmedical therapy and a more comprehensive approach to their disease. Some others empower the body with spirits and health. There are like four components probably that bring up the spirituality and the reaction of the patient toward their disease, the body, the health, their spirit, and their mind; they are all interconnected. There are many ways to address the spirituality. There is limited knowledge and training about how to approach the faith and the holiness of the patient.

The spirituality brought to the arena of medicine is still a difficult subject to deal with for most of the physicians. The physician needs to be sensitive to each patient as a person, this requires maintaining their hope, expressing interest, and exploring fears and doubts with the patient. This will facilitate the restoration of faith, the recovery of the patient within the hospital, within the community, and create a better work relationship with the patient thenself. Awareness about our religious and spiritual resources can improve the outcomes if there is a communication between the physician and patient. Sometimes just listening to the patient is sufficient. A decrease in stress, ability to meditate, ability to take the time to pray which can, in turn, be in meditation, could be a positive impact on the incidents of certain cardiovascular diseases. Therefore, the physician is to seek fundamental understanding of spiritual needs, resources, and preference, respect patient mental care, avoid promoting or discourage the specific spiritual practice and explore his or her spirituality and biases. But the most important is to practice without prejudice.

Wellness

Wellness is complicated and problematic. Swarbrick[1] showed how welfare is a compound of eight different elements.

> The first element, of course, is emotional. Efficiently coping with life and creating satisfaction in relations is the key to having a life balance.
>
> The second is financial. Satisfaction with the current and future economic situations is important because sometimes the patient can be unbalanced, and therefore, can be emotional.
>
> The third is social. Developing a sense of connection belonging to a well-developed support system is essential for the wellness of the patient.
>
> The fourth is spiritual. It includes expanding our sense of purpose and the meaning of life through things like spirituality, issues, and faith.
>
> The fifth is occupational. Personal satisfaction and enrichment derived from their work.
>
> The sixth is physical. Recognizing the need for physical activity, diet, nutrition, and all the natural remedies that can increase our wellness as a person during everyday life.
>
> The seventh is intellectual. Recognizing creativity and ability, and finding ways to expand knowledge and skill and keeping the mind busy is for some people the most important asepct for wellness of the whole body.
>
> The eight is environment. Good health by occupying pleasant areas in a well-supported environment without any risks.

Physician Role and Ethics Issues

Some physicians think they are obligated to present all the options to their patients including the spiritual one but 70% of the physicians believe that another physician will do that for them.

There are several ethics issues that can improve the outcome of the patient.

1. *Respect Religion.* Respect the religion and the belief of the patient. It has been shown that the outcomes of patients are more strongly associated with those with high levels of intrinsic religiosity. Respecting religion is of utmost importance nowadays given the many faiths present throughout the population and how to care for all of them. In general, a belief in any religion helps the patient to get better.

   Spirituality should be implemented to define and appropriately address a patient who can suffer for moral injury during the hospitalization, and this is where the role of the chaplain or similar for each religion can be of utmost importance.

2. *Respect time with the patient.* For sure, physicians can improve the time management. Some patients need time with the physician and for a physician to educate them on wellness and offer spiritual feedback or resources available in the hospital. We need, as a physician, more education and training toward the welfare of the patient that includes spirituality. We, as physicians, need to gain experience, training, and communication skills to overcome barriers to wellness and spirituality.

3. *Specialized hospital team.* We need a group in a hospital that can utilize community resources and treat the person and not just the disease of the patient. This is true especially at the end-of-life issues in oncology patients etc. The physician and the nurses should have a central role in treating these issues.

4. *End of life.* Physicians and nurses are in a unique position in the health care setting. Nurses can build trusting therapeutic relationships with their patients, different than other health care professionals. The nurse–physician team should be an integral part of the conversations about end-of-life care that include values, beliefs, desires, and fears of the patient and their families. It is suggested by the research, that there is an ethical justification for respecting autonomy and being beneficent regarding the end-of-life care for the health care professional. "Seriously ill people need end-of-life options. It is a basic human right to live and die with one's dignity intact."

5. *Conflict of interest.* Unfortunately, there are ethical issues, conflict of religions, standards of practice and legal issues that sometimes can come between the physician and the patient. All we can do at this point is to be sensitive to each person. Take care of them and offer appropriate care and services.

6. *Do Not Lie.* We need to maintain a patient's hope if we can but not lie to them. I know of a physician that would tell everybody they would live forever, even if they were in stage-IV cancer. Most of those patients ended up dying within a week. That is not fair to the family or the patient, nor is it ethical.

7. *Respect their wishes.* We need, when patients are suffering, to express interest in who they are, understand their fears and doubts and facilitate the healing of the patient within their family and within the community. For doing that, the physician probably needs to seek a basic understanding of the patient's spiritual need, resources, and preference. Respect the wishes of the spiritual care or the wishes of the patient, not just the one written down. Avoid discouraging of religious practice and be authentic.

8. *Be authentic.* If we need to pick one action, it is to be authentic with our patients and treat them as another person and not just as another patient. Medicine is a service profession, and therefore, relationship in coping is significant for helping to cure the patient.

Based on Previous Publication

Frezza, E. E. & Frezza G. E. 2017. Spirituality and wellness in medicine. An ethical task. *Annals of Yoga and Physical Therapy.* 2 (3): 1029–31.

Note

1. Swarbrick, M. 2006. A wellness approach. Psychiatric Rehabilitation Journal 29(4): 311–14.

Suggested Reading

1. Guerra A. L., E. E. Frezza. 2017. To die or not to die: this is the dilemma! *Journal of Epidemiology and Public Health (JEPHR)* 2(1): 150–3. ISSN 2471-8211. http://dx.doi.org/10.16966/2471-8211.138.
2. Hodgson T. J., and L. B. Carey. 2017. Moral injury and definitional clarity: betrayal, spirituality and the role of chaplains. *J. Rel. Health* 56(4): 1212–28..
3. How Can Faith Heal? *Time Magazine.* February 23, 2009.
4. Koenig, H. G. 2011. *Spirituality and Health research.* West Conshohocken, PA: Templeton press.
5. Peres M. F. P., H. H. Kamei, R. R. Tobo, and G. Lucchetti. 2017. Mechanism behind religiosity and spirituality's effect on mental health, quality of life and well-being. *J. Rel. Health* 400–6.

Ethics Summary Table

How to Introduce Spirituality and Wellness

Faith is an essential human force.
God is a tangible and intangible feeling.
Respect other faiths or preferences.
Physician needs to be sensitive to religion, and that can help for better care.
Person satisfying is connected to faith body balance and life balance.
Creativity and patient care are part of physician wellness.
Physician needs to be authentic.
Respecting others means others must respect you.
Medicine is a relationship of coping.

Chapter 20

Physician Leader and Satisfaction

Physician Appreciation

A discussion about physician appreciation and recognition is elaborate. Like most people, physicians would like to be appreciated for their personal and professional contributions.

At the same time, many physicians feel that "the Golden Age" of medicine is past and that they are in fact underappreciated by a society which accords celebrity status and outlandish wealth to athletes, actors, and "pop icons."

Physicians are reeling from an overhauled health care system, which is run for the most part by nonphysicians and continues to devalue physician efforts while rewarding the CEOs of large Health Care Corporations with ever-increasing compensation packages. Reimbursement of medical care, the "deliverable" of our health system, is considered an "expense" that interferes with the profits of the insurance industry. The major bedrock of physician appreciation, the response of a grateful patient, has been eroded in a system which interposes the "payor" between the doctor and the patient. In these times, one may indeed wonder how the physician is recognized for his or her contributions and whether, in fact, there is an appreciation for the considerable effort physicians exert to attain and maintain a level of professional excellence.

Gratitude and Recognition

To discuss the issue of recognition and appreciation, we need first to consider the forces that influence physician satisfaction.

Medicine is a service profession, whose practitioners are pledged to improve the well-being of others. Each new physician acknowledges this fact when reciting the "Hippocratic Oath" whether in its ancient or one of its more contemporary forms. This view of medicine is deeply ingrained in the consciousness of our society and forms the basis on which individuals contemplate a medical career.

To maintain independence and control, physicians are willing to work harder than many other individuals and are willing to defer immediate concrete rewards for more evanescent and sometimes more abstract gratification.

Central to physician's satisfaction is a sense that he or she is appreciated, recognized and respected for their achievements, past and present. For the practicing physician, acknowledgment by a grateful patient, student, or respected colleague are the most common everyday measures of satisfaction. Sometimes no external support is necessary, merely one's own recognition that a problematic diagnostic riddle was solved, or a vital experiment completed is sufficient.

Group recognition is essential, but not in itself sufficient for most physicians. Ensuring recognition of individual physician contributions in a meaningful way is vital. This should occur within the day to day environment in which the physician works.

Finance Not a Factor

Many articles on physician satisfaction indicate that monetary rewards are less critical to doctors than things which make their day to day life more accessible (i.e., gave them more control). Given the level of compensation most physicians can generate from their professional efforts, monetary incentives would need to be quite significant to make a real difference to physician satisfaction or behavior and would likely not be affordable across a large organization on a regular basis. To improve overall physician satisfaction within a team, it would seem more important to focus on enhancing factors that impact the physician's day to day life (parking, lounge, dining room, computer access) than only monetary inducements.

This includes an efficient working environment with adequate support staff and reliable information services. From the physician's perspective, this is one aspect of recognizing their worth.

Leadership

It is challenging to define leadership in medicine.

Leaders are those who organize "labor" into efficient units and monitor the distribution and use of capital assets and its progress. The leaders continue to monitor and evaluate progress adjusting along the way to ensure the improvement is maintained and efficiency is increased wherever possible. People are leaders in different ways.

Types of Leadership Style

The kinds of leadership styles can be summarized into three categories:

1. *Autocratic*: The autocratic leader makes decisions without reference to anyone else. There is a high degree of dependency on the leader; this approach can demotivate and alienate staff. It may be considered valuable in some types of business where decisions need to be made quickly and decisively.
2. *Democratic*: Democracy encourages decision making from a variety of perspectives, utilizing a process of consultation before decisions are taken. In this environment, leadership may be emphasized throughout an organization. The persuasive leader makes decisions and seeks to persuade others that the decision is correct. The democratic style may help to motivate and involve others, fostering a feeling of ownership in the firm, development of ideas, etc. While it improves the sharing of ideas and experiences within the business, it can delay decision making. Democracy is congruous to any company that relies on creativity and good interpersonal relations and excellent teamwork.
3. *Paternalistic*: The paternal leader acts as a "father figure" in which the leader makes the decisions. However, unlike the autocratic leader, the fatherly leader may consult with others and believes in the need to support staff.

Physician Retention

To hire and to retain personnel is becoming quite challenging. The average cost to replace a critical care nurse is about $50,000. The nurse turnover rate was around 20% between 2001–2004 and has now increased to above 20%. To replace a physician is four times more!

The second problem to take into consideration is malpractice risk. This is also probably secondary to dissatisfaction among patients, and it seems to be becoming more critical compared to many years ago. How many times during hospital stays did the doctor treat you with kindness and respect? Listen to you carefully? Explain things so that you could understand?

Quality of Services

These are some suggestions that have been placed online (www.medicare.com) for an assessment of health care providers. Therefore, quality and service are unfortunately becoming more inseparable. In fact, clinical quality is defined as delivering clinical care that is measurable and superior by recognized standards. Service excellence is meeting the needs and fulfilling expectations of patients and staff. Operational efficiency is doing both above efficiently without time or resource waste.

We live in a service economy today, and everyone is coming out with new services, the center of excellence, etc. The clinical results will overcome any other factors. Unfortunately, most patients today want to be treated like custom-ers. The most important thing is how you talk to them and how you treat them. I know some incredibly lovely people who have a lot of patients. On the other hand, you see some physicians who are excellent physicians, but they lack interpersonal skills; therefore, they have fewer patients than others. We cannot keep doing the same things and expect different results; there will be no progress, and as a result, changes will need to be made in our practice.

Setting goals is important:

- Time
- Labs
- Imaging results in the patient's charts at the time of rounds
- Inpatients discharged by noon
- OR cases starting on time
- Patients to be seen by a physician
- Any computer problems

The focus of our thinking is the word "care," such as quality of care for our patients, appreciation for what we do, responsiveness to our issues and efficiency of our practice. We need to focus on physician and patient satisfaction. Regular staff meetings with agenda items need to be implemented to discuss these issues.

New Leader in Medicine Will Focus on the Positive

Questions should include: What did the staff do well today? Try to:

1. See the positive in negative things.
2. Reiterate the positives by complimenting staff.
3. Identify the process of improvement areas where you can "work better together."
4. Make sure you have the tools and equipment to do the job.
5. Continue to coach the behavior performance and standard of care by making sure everyone understands the goals and expectations, and if they do not, find out what you can do to help.

This is an important issue because we need to identify the problems. It is impera-tive to have input to identify the issues from hospital personnel, patients, and physi-cians. For the patients, it can be the overall experience with the hospital or outpatient. For the physician, it can be the quality of life in your practice and if your practice is satisfying to you. From the staff, it can be identifying the input/output issues where difficulties arise during the day and to solve it. Give these tools to the physician and hospital so that this questionnaire can be used and identified to give feedback.

How Can You Help Physicians in Practice?

The following are the most important factors in the physician–team relationship:

1. Telephone log
2. Having information available when calling or returning calls to physicians
3. Patient locator log
4. Following policy of returning charts to chart slot or order rank
5. At least one thank-you card sent weekly to a physician

The goal of a leader is to create a team because the quarterback is an essential part of the team but will not win the game by himself.

Treat Colleagues as Customers

Give feedback either in writing or with an appreciation note. Create an endpoint with the physician where we all win. Make sure they know we will all win in this process.

Communications Between the Health Care Team

Effective communication is characterized by shared purpose and intent and collaboration. Team members value familiarity over formality. Health care team members need to trust each other and get a partnership growing for a common goal, providing the best care possible for their patients.

I believe there should be checks and double checks, accountable members, adequate supervision, and supervisor training. Equipment should be available and should be in line with what is available in comparable institutions; the team needs to learn how to use them. We should not just use fillers for a job, we need to have trained personal above all in health care, and outstanding health care is what we all strive for. Huddles, codes training, and codes of conduct should be reviewed on a regular basis. Team issues need to address their frustrations and concerns. Respect for team leaders needs to be emphasized and brought back.

The physician should assess the situation and make a recommendation according to *SBAR*:

- Situation
- Background
- Assessment
- Recommendation

The team leader should be identifying, and team spirit should be built. Roles should be assigned to each member as well as understanding the role and its limitation. Skill training should be available. Essential equipment should be available for the hospitals and team and physician. Safety and monitor outcome should be implemented.

The issues of the task should be assessed by the following technique:

STICC: Situation Task Intent Concern Calibrate.

This structured briefing protocol, used by a firefighter, is based on five steps:

1. *Situation*: Here is what I think we face.
2. *Task*: Here is what I think we should do.
3. *Intent*: Here is why.
4. *Concerned*: Here is what we should keep our eye on.
5. *Calibrate*: Talk to me. Tell me if you don't understand. What can I do?

Suggested Reading

1. Center for Creative Leadership. 2016. What Are the Characteristics of a Good Leader? April 17. Accessed at URL: https://www.ccl.org/blog/characteristics-good-leader-2/.
2. Chen, K.-C. 2012. Machine-to-machine communications for healthcare. *Journal of Computing Science and Engineering* 6 (2): 119–26. http://central.oak.go.kr/journallist/journaldetail.do?article_seq=11644&tabname=abst&resource_seq=-1&keywords=null.
3. Drummond, D. (n.d.). Physician Leadership Skills – 3 Reasons Doctors Make Poor Leaders and What You Can Do About It. Accessed at URL: https://www.thehappymd.com/blog/bid/290715/physician-leadership-skills-3-reasons-doctors-make-poor-leaders-and-what-you-can-do-about-it.
4. Inspire Your People. 2018. What Is Lead Simply? Accessed at URL: https://www.inspireyourpeople.com/leadership-qualities/?utm_source=google&utm_medium=cpc&utm_content=+-+Leadership+Qualities&utm_campaign=leadership+qualities&gclid=EAIaIQobChMIwOuV57Ge2QIVErXACh3P7gRxEAAYASAAEgLVnPD_BwE.
5. Kornacki, M. J. 2017. Three Starting Points for Physician Leadership, August 7. Accessed at URL: https://catalyst.nejm.org/three-starting-points-physician-leadership/.
6. McCulloch, P., J. Rathbone, and K. Catchpole. 2011. Interventions to improve teamwork and communications among healthcare staff. *BJS* 98 (4): 469–79.
7. NHS Solutions. 2017. Important Qualities of Leadership in the Healthcare Industry, June 3. Accessed at URL: http://nhss.com/important-qualities-of-leadership-in-the-healthcare-industry/.
8. Price, G. and Norbeck, T. 2017. Physician Leaders will Shape the Future of Medicine. *Forbes*. Accessed at URL: https://www.forbes.com/sites/physiciansfoundation/2017/09/06/physician-leaders-will-shape-the-future-of-medicine/#52ca06a42766.

9. Ray, W. and Norbeck, T. 2017. Physician leaders will shape the future of medicine. *Public Health*, September 6. Accessed at URL: https://www.forbes.com/sites/physiciansfoundation/2017/09/06/physician-leaders-will-shape-the-future-of-medicine/#45711cfe2766.

10. Rosen, A., M. A. Stuchly, and A. Vander Vorst. 2002. Applications of RF/microwaves in medicine. *IEEE Trans. microwave Theory Tech* 50: 963–74. Accessed at URL: http://scholar.google.com/scholar_url?url=http://ieeexplore.ieee.org/abstract/document/989992/&hl=en&sa=X&scisig=AAGBfm2F0FTg2-yQDp0aUbOQilZFvtaKYg&nossl=1&oi=scholarr.

11. Saunders, C., and Hagemann, B. 2009. Physicians as leaders: what's missing? *Media Health Leaders*, April 15, Accessed at URL: http://www.healthleadersmedia.com/physician-leaders/physicians-leaders-whats-missing.

12. The Becker Hospital Review. 2015. 5 Important Qualities for a Medical Leader (and One to Avoid), September 15. Accessed at URL: https://www.beckershospitalreview.com/hospital-management-administration/5-important-qualities-for-a-medical-leader-and-one-to-avoid.html.

Ethics Summary Table

How to be a Satisfied Physician Leader

Physicians like to be appreciated.

Hospitals and health care systems should recognize the physician role.

Physicians should be in more leader positions.

Gratitude is required, but it is not given from both patient and administration.

Dissatisfaction is related to details of daily physician life.

A small amount of change can improve team feeling.

Learn to be a leader.

Satisfaction is related to physician retainment.

Setting goals to improve quality of services.

Focus on the positive.

Raise from the negative to find the solution.

Be a leader and support your fellow colleagues.

Apply structure from briefing protocol.

SBAR: (1) Situation, (2) Background, (3) Assessment, (4) Recommendation.

STICC: (1) Situation, (2) Task, (3) Intent, (4) Concern, (5) Calibrate.

Chapter 21

Divorce Rate Among Physicians

Lawsuit and Divorces

Divorce rates among doctors vary according to specialty.[1]

While the everyday stresses of a physician's life may not contribute to the divorce rate all that much, a lawsuit can change that dramatically. The divorce rate among physicians who are being sued is ninety percent.

The financial realities change drastically during and after a lawsuit, and the family may not be able to maintain the life to which they have grown accustomed. The change is often sudden, as was the case in our marriage, and it is hard not to feel as if you're under attack from all sides when in the middle of such turmoil. Family cannot deal with the importance of the lawsuit, with the publicity, or with the lack of income; they are used to a different and beautiful lifestyle.

Some partners accustomed to certain perks will not last long when these perks are taken away. They do not know how to deal with a lawsuit; love comes second given the high levels of stress, and the couple breaks down.

In the presence of a more balanced life, Dr. Anupam Jena and Dr. Dan Ly investigated the divorce among physicians, and they found, surprisingly, that doctors have one of the lowest rates of divorce among health care professionals. They conclude their article by saying: "It's been speculated that doctors are more likely to be divorced than other professionals because of the long hours they keep and the stress associated with the job, but no large-scale study has ever investigated whether that is true. We found that doctors have among the lowest rates of divorce among health care professionals." Stress and emotion can impact this statistic.

Emotional Detachment

Emotional detachment is a problem for everybody, including physicians. This has also been reported on posts on Facebook.[2]

On the emotional detachment page on Wikipedia,[3] I like the way Wikipedia reported this issue:

- Emotional detachment often arises from *psychological trauma* and is a component of many anxieties and stress disorders. The person, while physically present, moves elsewhere in their mind, and in a sense is "not entirely present," making them sometimes appear preoccupied.
- Thus, such detachment is often not as outwardly visible as other psychiatric symptoms; people with this problem often have emotional systems that are in overdrive. They may have a hard time being a loving family member.
- They may avoid activities, places, and people associated with any traumatic events they have experienced. The dissociation can also lead to lack of attention and, hence, to memory problems and in extreme cases, amnesia.
- Divorce is the end of the road.

The Implication as Physician

Again from the article of Dr. Anupam Jena and Dr. Dan Ly,[1] they analyzed the results of surveys of more than 40,000 doctors and 200,000 nurses, pharmacists, dentists, and health care executives, conducted between 2008 and 2013.

Those who said they'd been divorced included 23% of pharmacists, 24% of doctors, 25% of dentists, 31% of health care executives and 33% of nurses.

The researchers also looked at people who work outside the health field and found that 35% of them had been divorced.

Among doctors, women were about 1.5 times more likely to have been divorced than men of a similar age. Female doctors who worked more than 40 hours a week were more likely to be divorced than those who worked fewer hours, while the reverse was true among male doctors.

Study lead author Dr. Dan Ly explained in the press release, "We believe that the higher incidence of divorce among female physicians stems from the greater tradeoffs they are forced to make to achieve work/life balance.

"More research is needed to understand whether that interpretation is indeed accurate and, if it is, what can be done to help with work/life balance," he added.

Specialties and Psychological Traits

Physician divorce rates vary by specialty and psychological traits.[4] According to the University of the Pittsburgh web page:

1. Divorce rates among physicians vary according to specialty and psychological traits. However, they are not affected by a host of other factors, including gender, which previously was thought to be relevant according to a study by Pitt assistant professor Bruce L. Rollman.[5]
2. The overall cumulative rate of divorce among 1,118 physicians was 29% by 30 years of marriage. Rollman found that psychiatrists had the highest divorce rate, 50%, followed by surgeons, 33%. For internists, pediatricians, and pathologists the rates ranged from 22 to 24%.
3. Some psychological variables also proved crucial. Physicians who scored in the highest quarter on a test measuring anger had a 44% incidence of divorce compared with 27% for the rest of the study group. Perceiving one's self as having been less emotionally close with one's parents also was associated with a higher divorce rate.
4. Rollman's study debunked other factors previously thought to affect divorce among physicians, including gender, depression, religion, medical school class rank, being an only child, parental history of divorce and having a parent or parents who were physicians. While women physicians had a higher absolute incidence of divorce (37 versus 28%), after adjusting for other factors, such as specialty, female physicians had the same risk of divorce as male physicians.

Pediatricians try to be warm and friendly, but at the same time, they miss their own family issues.

When asked to guess which specialty had the highest divorce rate, most physicians said surgeons, who actually had the second highest rate.

In an article in the *New England Journal of Medicine*, B.L. Rollman and co-authors cite Dr. Nada Stotland's observations: "Surgeons are never home," she reported. "They're abused in their training; it's extremely hierarchical, they're used to giving orders and having them unquestioningly obeyed. Not all spouses are into being surgical nurses."[5]

Rollman drew on the Johns Hopkins Precursors Study, which tracked 1,337 people who entered the Johns Hopkins University School from 1944 through 1960. That group included only 8% female physicians, 2% Asians, and no African-Americans. Excluding those who did not graduate, as well as those for whom marital and divorce information was incomplete, Rollman's study was based on 1,118 married physicians and reported in the *New England Journal of Medicine*.[5]

How Often Divorce Takes Place in the United States

According to Wilkinson and Finkbeiner, as of 2016[6]

- Almost 50% of all marriages in the United States will end in divorce or separation.
- Researchers estimate that 41% of all first marriages end in divorce.
- 60% of all second marriages end in divorce.
- 73% of all third marriages end in divorce.
- The United States has the 6th highest divorce rate in the world.
- Both marriage rates and divorce rates in the United States are decreasing.
- The marriage rate in the United States is currently 6.8 per 1,000 total population.
- The divorce rate in the United States is 3.2 per 1,000 population (as of 2014, the latest year of data from the Centers for Disease Control (CDC), with 44 states and DC reporting). This is known as the "crude divorce rate." Although useful for describing changes in divorce rates over time, the crude divorce rate does not provide accurate information on the percentage of first marriages that end in divorce.

According to the same group of lawyers:

- Over a 40-year period, 67% of first marriages terminate.
- Among all Americans 18 years of age or older, whether they have been married or not, 25% have gone through a marital split.
- 15% of adult women in the United States are divorced or separated today, compared with less than 1% in 1920.
- The average first marriage that ends in divorce lasts about 8 years.

Professions with highest divorce rate:

- Dancers – 43%
- Bartenders – 38.4%
- Massage Therapists – 38.2%
- Gaming Cage Workers – 34.6%
- Gaming Service Workers – 31.3%
- Food and Tobacco Machine Operators – 29.7%
- Telephone Operators – 29.3%
- Textile Machine Operators – 29%
- Physicians – 28.9%
- Nurses – 28.7%

The same group of authors also discuss why people are divorcing in the United States. A lack of commitment is the most common reason given by divorcing couples according to a recent national survey. Here are the reasons that were given and their percentages:

- Lack of commitment 73%
- Argue too much 56%
- Infidelity 55%

Professions with lowest divorce rate:

- Medical Scientists – 9.11%
- Other Scientists – 8.79%
- Legislators – 8.74%
- Audiologists – 7.77%
- Dentists – 7.75%
- Farmers – 7.63%
- Podiatrists – 6.81%
- Clergy – 5.61%
- Optometrists – 4.01%
- Agricultural Engineers – 1.78%

Finances affect divorce rates; an annual income of over $50,000 can decrease the risk of divorce by as much as 30% versus those with a salary of under $25,000. Feeling that one's spouse spent money foolishly increased the likelihood of divorce 45% for both men and women.

The Toll a Divorce Takes

A new study entitled "Divorce and Death"[7] show that broken marriages can kill at the same rate as smoking cigarettes. Indications that the risk of dying is a full 23% higher among divorcées than married people.

One researcher determined that a single divorce costs state and federal governments about $30,000 based on such things as the higher use of food stamps and public housing as well as increased bankruptcies and juvenile delinquency.

The nation's 1.4 million divorces in 2002 are estimated to have cost the taxpayers more than $30 billion.

An article in the *New York Times* stated that – of couples who seek marriage counseling – 38% end up divorced just two years later.

Notes

1. Ly, D.P. et al. 2015. Divorce among physicians and other healthcare professionals in the United States: Analysis of census survey data. *BMJ* 350. doi: https://doi.org/10.1136/bmj.h706.
2. Help4living – Posts. Facebook. Accessed at URL: https://www.facebook.com/help4living/posts.
3. Wikipedia. 2016. Emotional Detachment. Accessed at URL: https://en.wikipedia.org/wiki/Emotional_detachment.
4. Research Notes. (1997, May 1). The University Times. Accesses at URL: https://www.utimes.pitt.edu/archives/?p=5326.
5. Rollman, B. et al. 1997. Medical specialty and the incidence of divorce. *N Engl J Med.* 336: 800–803.
6. Wilkinson & Finkbeiner. 2017. Divorce Facts and Statistics: What Affects Divorce Rates? Accessed at URL: http://www.wf-lawyers.com/divorce-statistics-and-fact.
7. Lamar, M. 2017. Divorce is Like Death Without the Support or Rituals. *The Huffington Post.* Accessed at URL: https://www.huffingtonpost.com/michelle-lamar/divorce-is-like-death-wit_b_781025.html.

Ethics Summary Table

How to Read the Increase in the Divorce Rate

Routine physician life is not connected to an increase in the divorce rate.

The risk of divorce is raised by emotional detachment and lawsuits.

Female physicians have a higher rate of separation than male physicians.

Specialties play a role.

Psychiatrist and surgeons have the highest rate of divorce (50% and 33%).

Surprisingly, pediatricians and internist have a 20% rate of divorce.

If you ask a physician, they would say surgeons have the highest risk of divorce.Surgeons are abused during training and are always on call.

In the United States 50% of first marriages end in divorce, 60% of second marriages, and 73% of third marriages.

Cost of divorce in the United States: 30 billion dollars.

Chapter 22

Stress and Suicide

Stress and Burnout

Physical complications of increased pressure are well-known. These include insomnia, gastrointestinal disturbance, tension headaches, hypertension, fatigue, lowered immunity, menstrual irregularities, and sexual dysfunction. Adverse effects of stress may affect not only the individual doctor but also his/her family life, marriage, and social life. Furthermore, stress is associated with burnout.[1]

The physician has a lower mortality risk from cancer and heart disease relative to the general population (presumably related to knowledge of self-care and early diagnosis), but they have a significantly higher risk of dying from suicide. Suicide is the most common cause of death among medical students.

It has been known for more than 150 years that physicians have an increased propensity to die by suicide. It was estimated in 1977 that on average the United States loses the equivalent of approximately 300–400 physicians/year, a doctor a day.[2] The medical profession consistently stays near the top of the list of occupations with the highest risk of death by suicide.

Depression is at least as standard in the medical profession as in the general population, affecting an estimated 12% of males and up to 19.5% of females.

Depression is even more common in medical students and residents, with 15–30% of them screening positive for depressive symptoms. This is also common in other countries such as, Finland, Norway, Australia, Singapore, China, Taiwan, and Sri Lanka.

Litigation-related stress can precipitate depression and occasionally suicide. Some physicians have committed suicide upon the first receipt of malpractice claims, after judgments against them in court, or after financially motivated settlements foisted upon them by a malpractice insurer solely to cut the insurer's losses. Any agreement in a malpractice case is by law reported to the National Practitioner

Data Bank, which is yet another source of distress and stigma that can contribute to depression.[3]

Physicians who have reported depressive symptoms (even those for which they are receiving adequate treatment) to their licensing boards, potential employers, hospitals, and other credentialing agencies have experienced a range of adverse consequences. These included loss of their medical privacy and autonomy, repetitive and intrusive examinations, licensure restrictions, discriminatory employment decisions, practice restrictions, hospital privilege limitations, and increased supervision.

Fear of Reporting

However, because of the stigma associated with depression, self-reporting likely underestimates the prevalence of the disease in medical populations. It is also a leading risk factor for myocardial infarction in male and female physicians, and it may play a role in immune suppression, thus, increasing the risk of many infectious diseases and cancer.[3]

Physicians feel an obligation to appear healthy, perhaps as evidence of their ability to heal others. The concerned colleague or partner may say nothing while wondering privately if the colleague has become impaired.

Medical licensure applications and renewal applications frequently require answers to broad-based, time-unlimited questions regarding the physician's mental health history without regard to current impairment, and courts have determined that they are impermissible, because the resultant examinations and restrictions constitute discrimination under Title II of the Americans with Disabilities Act (ADA) based on stereotypes.

Physicians also fear losing hospital privileges if treatment for depression is disclosed. Hospital administrators increasingly use mandated psychiatric treatment as a bullying tactic to remove independent-thinking, patient-focused physicians from hospital staff.

Because many states require reporting by other licensed physicians of a physician who may be suffering from a potentially impairing condition, physicians can be reluctant to seek treatment from colleagues, or from utilizing their insurance coverage, or even from using their names when seeking treatment. A physician whose thought processes are clouded by depression and the anticipated consequences of seeking treatment for it may honestly believe that self-treatment is the only safe option.

Suicide Facts and Figures

Physicians, in general, have a higher rate of suicide than other professional groups and the public. Women physicians' suicide rates are reported to be up to 400% higher than women in other professions. Male physicians' rates are 50%–70% higher. These figures were taken from *Physician News Digest* and written by Elizabeth Lee Vliet.[4]

MDD:

- Major depressive disorder (MDD) affects 13–17% of Americans every year.
- The rate of MDD in physicians is like that of the general population: 13% of male physicians and 20% of female physicians.
- One-third of medical residents have a diagnosable MDD during residency.
- 30% of physicians show MDD one year after graduation.
- MDD is a risk factor for suicide.

Suicide is:

- Seventh leading cause of death in U.S. men.
- Fifth leading cause of death in U.S. women.
- Third leading cause of death for Americans aged 15–24.
- Most prevalent in elderly and adolescents.
- Highest rate: Men over 85.
- Physician health experts say as many as 400 U.S. physicians take their lives each year.
- Physicians who make suicide attempts are much more likely to complete suicide than non-physicians.
- The rate of death in male physicians is 70% higher, and the rate in female physicians is 250%–400% higher than the general population.

Why are Physicians at Risk?

The medical profession is perceived as a very stressful occupation. Although some stressors in health care settings are inevitable and invariable, such as dealing with incurable patients and their dying, some variable workplace stressors represent a risk for medical professionals. The work organization, financial issues, administration, interference with family and social life, relationships with colleagues and patients, and work demand (long working hours, workload, and pressure).

These are some trigger points:

- Demands of profession and patients
- Lack of sleep
- Poor eating habits and level of fitness
- Exposure to illness, tragedy, and death
- Oversight
- Access to medication
- Burnout
- Medical profession implicitly discourages help-seeking in its members.

- Physicians with psychiatric diseases often encounter discrimination in medical licensing, hospital privileges, health insurance, professional liability insurance, and professional advancement.
- 35% of physicians do not have a regular source of health care.

Doctors have always been at higher risk of suicide than other professions for several reasons:[4]

- Pressures of responsibility for patients' lives
- Fear of making mistakes that might cost a life or trigger a malpractice lawsuit
- Fear of losing one's medical license and livelihood
- Long hours, time away from families on nights and weekends
- High rates of unrecognized or untreated depression, alcohol or substance abuse, and divorce due to all of the above.

Reactions to a Lawsuit

- Mourning
- Systemic anxiety
- Guilt and blame
- Anger and rage at the deceased
- Business as usual
- Broken contract
- Sense of betrayal, abandonment
- Severed relationship
- Interruption in health care delivery
- Anger
- Burden of trust issues for next physician

The most challenging thing for a physician is that he is considered guilty until proven innocent! That is what it feels like to be accused of something in the USA. No, I didn't go to jail, but if I had been seen as innocent, I wouldn't have lost everything I'd built up either. Innocent until proven guilty should be the norm, not the exception. Everybody looks at you like you're a criminal. It doesn't matter if the problem is someone else's. It doesn't matter if the accusation is false. It doesn't even matter if the charge isn't all that damning. Once people start looking at you like you're a pariah, you're a pariah.

Why Choose Suicide?

- Fulfill the desire to die
- Escape from an intolerable situation
- Get relief from a difficult state of mind

- Get relief from intractable pain
- Avoid loss of control
- Make people understand how desperate they were feeling

Risk Factors

- Age (adolescent/elderly)
- Male gender
- Unmarried
- Caucasian
- Stigma
- Access to medications or firearms
- Impulsive behavior
- Family history of suicide
- Mental disorders or substance abuse
- Family violence including physical and sexual abuse
- Feelings of hopelessness
- Cultural and religious beliefs

Suicidal ideation is strongly related to:

- Burnout
    - Emotional exhaustion
    - Depersonalization
    - Low personal accomplishment
- Perceived significant medical error in last three months

No one talks about suicide – especially in the medical community.

There is widespread agreement about an immediate need for increased discussion and preventive measures for physicians about the topic of suicide, beginning in medical school and continuing through their entire professional career.[5]

Why is the Practice Burning Out Physicians?

Why do more physicians see suicide as their only option? The rising rate after the 2010 Affordable Care Act was passed, points to the added regulatory and financial pressures from Obamacare[4] as significant factors:

- Need to see more patients per hour to make ends meet
- Lower payments, longer delays in being paid, and declining patient visits due to higher co-pays and deductibles

■ Financial stress, a known trigger for suicide, intensified by a 40–50% decline in practice revenues, as overhead costs go, forcing many primary care physicians to close up their practices

■ Increasing administrative and paperwork burden, which takes time away from patient care without the satisfaction of helping patients

■ More generalized "one-size-fits-all" protocols demanded by insurance and government "guidelines"

■ More forms, reports, and regulations that no one understands, but with huge financial penalties and even prison time for making mistakes

■ The demonization of "greedy doctors" by insurance companies, government, and media

Doctors are human, too, and have feelings. Critical overlooked factors in the rising suicide rates since 2010 include:

■ The increasing sense that doctors are interchangeable with those with less training and expertise

■ Feeling unappreciated by patients, who toss them aside like an old toy when insurance plans change

■ Frustration with patients who dismiss medical recommendations if "it is not covered by my insurance"

■ Loss of autonomy, control, and independence as faceless insurance clerks, bean-counters, licensing boards, and government agencies dictate how, where, and when medicine is to be practiced, with no knowledge of the patient in question

Notes

1. Wong, J. G. W. S. 2008. Doctors and stress. *Medical Bulletin* 13(6): 4–7. The Federation of Medical Societies. Accessed from URL: http://www.fmshk.org/database/articles/03mb1_3.pdf.
2. Elizabeth, E. 2017. Famous Holistic Doctor & Wife Allegedly Jump to Death off Manhattan Office Highrise – Leave typed Suicide Notes, July 28. Health Nut News. Accessed from URL: https://www.healthnutnews.com/famous-holistic-doctor-wife-allegedly-jump-to-deat.
3. Andrew, L. B. 2017. Physician Suicide: Overview, Depression in Physicians. Medscape. Accessed from URL: http://emedicine.medscape.com/article/806779-overview.
4. Vliet, E. L. 2014. Physician suicide rates have climbed since Obamacare. *Physician News Digest*. Accessed from URL: https://physiciansnews.com/2015/05/19/physician-suicide-rates-have-climbed-since.
5. Myers, M. 2018. Suicide in Physicians: Toward Prevention. Missouri Physician Health Program. Accessed from URL: http://www.themphp.org.

Ethics Summary Table

How to Read Stress And Burnout

Physicians have a higher chance of dying by suicide than general population.

It is the most common cause of death in medical students.

Depression affects 20% of women doctors.

Depression in doctors increases to 30% during their residency.

Litigations and lawsuits further unbalance physician's lives and the risk of suicide increases to 50% or more.

Male physicians are 50–70% more likely to commit suicide than the general population.

Female physicians are 400% more likely to commit suicide than general population.

Fear of reporting burnout and depression is the number one cause of suicide.

Physicians avoid cures for fear of losing their license and job.

There is no support system to cure physicians anonymously.

The burnout is effected by high demand from patients and the health care system.

Fear of mistakes, long hours, responsibility, excessive overlook from society, decrease income.

Lawsuits affect insurance rates, patient rating, family

Physician is guilty till proven otherwise contrary to the U.S. system (innocent till prove otherwise).

Physician has lost the autonomy to practice.

They experience emotional detachment.

Death is seen as a liberation.

QUALITY AND DIGNITY

Chapter 23

Common Ground
with Patients

Medical Quality

Medical quality is the degree to which health care systems, services, and supplies for individuals and populations increase the likelihood of positive health outcomes.

Clinical quality improvement is an interdisciplinary process designed to raise the standards of the delivery of preventive, diagnostic, therapeutic, and rehabilitative measures to maintain, restore, or improve health outcomes of individuals and populations.

Phillip Caper[1] defined the medical quality as the quality of medical care rendered by physicians in and outside of hospitals which has become a subject of increasing public and, more recently, private-sector concern. Until quite recently, third-party payers were reluctant to question the medical decisions of physicians, recognizing that medicine is a complex equation and that one of the hallmarks of a profession is self-regulation. Beyond the issue of professional autonomy, though, is the reality that "quality" is defined differently by different interests. In this paper, Philip Caper discusses the evolution of federal involvement in the pursuit of quality, noting that organized medicine has never been bashful about employing the quality argument to thwart health policy thrusts that it opposed.

Better Quality = Better Care

How can we provide better care and professionalism?

Quality is the tool through which both the professionalism and the relationship with patients and another physician is measured. To maintain quality, care needs to be provided according to basic standards which is founded on the following:

- Improving quality of care
- Improving access to care
- Just distribution of finite resources
- Commitment to scientific knowledge
- Maintaining trust by managing conflicts of interest
- Commitment to professional responsibilities

Shared Goals

Dr. F. Kleisinger suggested making sure that the physician and the patient have a shared understanding of the importance of the medical problem in question, of the availability of adequate treatments for this issue, and of the risks if the problem remains untreated or undertreated.

This shared understanding is the foundation on which all treatment contracts are based. Start by asking how the patient understands the medical condition and why it needs treatment. Ask if the patient has any concerns or questions about the recommended procedures, lifestyle modifications, diagnostic tests, or follow-up and monitoring plans.[2]

Ask if there is an alternative approach that the patient has been using or considering. Allow time for this process because whatever the patient tells you can be invaluable for tailoring your approach to improving compliance.

Ask the patient for his or her analysis of the roots of the problems. Ask what strategies the patient might suggest for addressing the issue. Dr. Kleisinger proposed some open-ended, nonjudgmental questions, which are very useful in this situation:

"What could I do differently to help you with this?"
"How could we approach this problem more effectively?"
"What are the obstacles that have prevented our dealing with this more successfully?"

The very act of asking these questions can help reframe the situation from a combative one to a more collaborative one. Be aware that guilt, shame, or a sense of failure is common particularly when diseases are seriously threatening the patient's health. Your open, nonaccusatory, and problem-solving stance will help defuse these negative emotions.

Cause of patient non-adherence:

- Denial
- Depression
- Dementia
- Cultural issues
- Drug abuse
- Financial cost of treatment

Ask the patient to describe how s/he understands his or her medical disorder in his or her own words.

Ask if the patient understands the purpose of treatment and the consequences of ineffective therapy.

Have the patient explain the specific treatment recommendations upon which you agree in detail.

Using open-ended questions, ask if the patient feels confident in following the treatment recommendations and if the patient sees any problems.

Work to mutually find solutions to any issues with compliance that are identified.

American Medical Association (AMA) Focus Training

There are training sessions offered by the AMA and other organizations, but we like to suggest more focused and real-time training such as:

1. Advanced communication skills for physician
2. Admitting mistakes: Ethical and communication
3. Working across language and cultures: The case for informed consent
4. Working with professionals around you: Team communication
5. Delivering bad news – Your chance to become a master physician
6. The stress of practicing medicine

The specific educational goals and objectives of the six seminars are as follows:

1. Relationship building.
2. Patient education/information giving.
3. Knowing the relevant ethical constructs underlying informed consent.
4. Knowing what to do.
5. Formally teaching communication skills with patients and colleagues, challenging us to define our personal and professional goals, and sharing the experience that we live in an inexact profession where perfection is a worthy – but unachievable – goal is the challenge of professionalism.

6. Having the courage to face these challenges in open forums with residents, junior faculty, and senior faculty is not only a requirement of the medical accrediting agencies but also the right thing to do.

Recently, honest attempts to coordinate the care of patients with complex health care needs have further stressed the previously fragile limits of patient confidentiality to the breaking point. Internet programs now permit hospital/city/region-wide access to a patient's medical record. The clear benefit to the patient and treating physician is to guarantee accurate retrieval and assessment of each patient's medications, allergies, and past medical history.

Notes

1. Caper, P. 1974. The meaning of quality in medical care. *N Engl J Med*, 291: 1136–1137.
2. Kleisenger, F. 2003. In *Medical Education and Ethics: Concepts, Methodologies, Tools, and Applications*. Mehdi Khosrow-Pour (Ed.). Hershey, PA: IGI. 986.

Suggested Reading

1. Agency for Health Care Policy and Quality. 2016. The Six Domains of Health Care Quality. Accessed at URL: https://www.ahrq.gov/professionals/quality-patient-safety/talkingquality/create/sixdomains.html.
2. Agency for HealthcareResearch and Quality. Understanding Quality Measurement. 2017. Accessed at URL: https://www.ahrq.gov/professionals/quality-patient-safety/quality-resources/tools/chtoolbx/understand/index.html.
3. American College Medical Quality. (n. d.). Policies. Accessed at URL: http://www.acmq.org/policies/policies1and2.pdf.
4. Claxton, G., C. Cox, S. Gonzales, R. Kamal, and L. Levitt. Measuring the Quality of Healthcare in the U.S. Kaiser Family Foundation. Accessed at URL: https://www.healthsystemtracker.org/brief/measuring-the-quality-of-healthcare-in-the-u-s/.
5. Stanford Health Care. 2018. Quality Care for Every Patient. Accessed at URL: https://stanfordhealthcare.org/about-us/quality.html.

Ethics Summary Table

How Share Ground with Patient

Share the treatment pathway
Bring brochures
Suggest searching on the web
Show the patient you are a quality physician
Share your plan
Ask patients what they understand

Ask the patient what the root of their problems is
Build relationships with the patient and their family
Look for patient non-adherence: Denial, depression, dementia, or drug abuse
Work across language and cultural differences
Coordinate care with the whole professional team

Chapter 24

Dementia and Dignity

Dementia

People with cognitive changes caused by Mild Cognitive Impairment (MCI) have an increased risk of developing Alzheimer's or dementia.

However, not all people with MCI develop Alzheimer's.[1]

The issue of dementia from an ethics point of view is to understand the needs of both the provider (physician, nurses, etc.) and the caregiver (family and proxy). The health care provider has some experience in treating people with dementia but the family may not. This may be their first time caring directly for a patient, and in this case the patient is a member of their family, a parent most of the time, or a husband, a wife, etc.

Therefore, we have the issues of the physician's practice ethical decision and behavior and the family, which was thrown into the field unexpectedly.

The patient is in the middle, and most of the time, we forget about him/her. The most important thing is that we do not lose focus on the dignity of the patient. Yes, the dignity of these people with cognitive impairment is of utmost importance.

MCI

Not all dementia is Alzheimer's and not all Alzheimer's stages and treatments will be the same for every patient, and this can be frustrating for medical professionals as it becomes increasingly difficult to single out cases and treat them appropriately.

Each patient will go through the stages of the disease at their own pace and some may find that they develop stages more quickly or more slowly than others.

There is no cure for Alzheimer's, but an early diagnosis can allow a person the opportunity to live well with the disease for as long as possible and plan for their future.

Challenges

Patients start having difficulties and try to hide them. My personal experience with my father is that he was protecting his disease well. When I discussed this with experts in the field, they told me that highly intelligent or efficient people could conceal their decreased cognitive problems quite well for a while; they know they have it, but they can hide it. This is the point where they start talking only of the past and bring up old memories as a way to hide that they do not remember the present.

These patients face the following challenges, which were retrieved from the Alzheimer's Association.[1]

1. Problems coming up with the right word or name
2. Trouble remembering names when introduced to new people
3. Challenges performing tasks in social or work settings
4. Forgetting material that one has just read
5. Losing or misplacing a valuable object
6. Increasing trouble with planning or organizing

Duty for the Professionals

During the late stages of dementia, the role of the caregiver is focused on preserving the quality of life and dignity of the patient. Although a person in the late stage of Alzheimer's typically loses the ability to talk and express needs, research tells us that some core of the person's self may remain. Some researchers said that we can communicate with them till the last stages of the disease.[2]

As reported by Julian Hughes,[3] the physician has several challenges:

- Assessment
- Community resources
- Confidentiality
- Lack of support
- Need for information
- Professionalism
- Relations with the patient's family
- Telling the patient the diagnosis

There is the potential problem that the "ethical" vocabulary used by professionals and family carers might be different, thus, leading to misunderstanding. A question about medication might require an ethical discussion, feelings of guilt might not be readily rationalized, and the need to go on caring might reflect a moral intuition involving reciprocity. Professionals need to be alert and sensitive to ethical issues for the family.[3]

Duty for the Family

Physicians need to explain to the family the stages of dementia and what will happen to the patient in each of them. We need to define at which stage they need to seek a hospice since at that point the patient won't be mobile and will have an unstable gait. These features are what I learned, from experience, about the stages of dementia:

Stage 1: No impairment
Stage 2: Mild cognitive decline
Stage 3: Same, plus difficulty focusing
Stage 4: Cognitive decline
Stage 5: Severe cognitive decline, lack of memory (need to keep an eye on them)
Stage 6: Severe activities decline, (eating and activities need to be monitored)
Stage 7: Worsening of stage 6 (eating, bathing, dressing, they will be unable to do any of these without supervision)

The last scene requires the most treatment and medication but is also the most hopeless stage, as patients may become unrecognizable when the body (the shell) is there, but the person is not responding. But people with dementia keep their identity to the end; even if they look like shell, they can feel and think.

The health care provider needs to educate the family with a common goal; the decision is about making sure the person receives the care needed.

The end or late stages of Alzheimer's disease can raise questions about the type of care offered to individuals in the final stages of a fatal illness. This statement provides information on the types of care available and stresses the importance of advance directives.

Aligning Providers and Family

It is of utmost importance that physicians and all their team explain and ask about the feelings and issues the family have about the diagnosis, disease stage, and medical strategy. Most often the focus is on the patient, and we forget about the family who need to cope with a person that, all the sudden, seems like a shell of their old self. It is like his soul is not there anymore, which is what it felt like to me with my Father.

I did not have any support; even though I was a physician, I did not know what to do, and I had to learn on my own on different web pages. My mother, who is not computer friendly, was left even more alone than me. What do you do when the patient wakes up in the middle of the night and tries to get you out of "his house" because he does not recognize you? My mother was locked out of the house and called the police to get back in. How can you calm a person down when they have hallucinations? Most of the time, they do not want to take the medications, or they hide them.

I never recognized my mother enough for a job which is usually done mostly by hospices.

The process is long and painful and you always have the hope that it will reverse, but the stages of Alzheimer are quite common and repeat themselves in different people.

The family most often feels:

- The notion of "conscience" as underpinning their duty to care
- Aligned with the sense of duty and responsibility and a sense of guilt
- The need to justify deceiving the person with dementia into believing different things with intent to help
- Reciprocity, by ignoring his previously expressed wishes
- Not appreciated for the strain of caring

I never realized the strain that a patient with cognitive impairment can bring on the family till I had my own experience.

Families living with Alzheimer's will face many decisions throughout the disease including decisions about care, treatment, participation in research, end-of-life issues, autonomy, and safety.

First, they do not realize how much care they need, and during the late stages, this can exceed what they can provide at home even with assistance.

The trauma of moving a person to a facility is on both sides – patient and family.

The decisions in the late stages are becoming more pressing and more difficult to make, and some families are not ready. They need to follow through, but they are always second guessing their initial decision.

Dignity of Care

At the end of life regardless of the disease, there are very few options. For people with cognitive impairment who cannot stay home because they became dangerous to themselves and others, the hospice is the only option.

The underlying philosophy of the hospice focuses on quality of life and dignity by providing comfort, care, and support services for people with terminal illnesses and their families. To qualify for hospice benefits under Medicare, a physician must diagnose the person with Alzheimer's disease as having less than six months to live.[2]

The focus is on having a sit-down discussion with the family and explaining the reasons medically and ethically. The best action will be talking to the patient themselves, if he still can understand, and share options about life-sustaining treatment.

As cognitive abilities decline, respect for the autonomy of the person with dementia will conflict with the ethical considerations of taking away a person's right to autonomous decision making.

The health care provider must also be trained in taking care of Alzheimer's patients; just showing up to work is not enough. The hospice needs to have specific training for the providers, and physicians should look at the quality care of these facilities. Often, the people that work in these services are not trained; they do not know what the disease can bring and most of all they lack compassion.

The health care providers also need to have the personnel to help to cope with Alzheimer's patients for the family members. One example is a couple that gets separated by the disease all of a sudden because of the condition; after many years together, it is a significant trauma for the one that is still sane and can create disease and psychological impairment to the one that needs to be strong and help the patient in this time of their life.

The health care system needs to be set in the way of understanding what is going on with the patient to cope and to give the best treatment which in this case started with the family.

All they need at the end of the stages is the dignity of care – that will be our ethical contract with them.

Notes

1. Alzheimer's Asssociation. Stages of Alzheimer's. Accessed at URL: https://www.alz.org/alzheimers-dementia/stages?type=alzchptfoot.
2. Alzheimer's Asssociation. Stages of Alzheimer's. Accessed at URL: https://www.alz.org/help-support/caregiving/stages-behaviors/late-stage.
3. Hughes, J. C. et al. 2002. Dementia and ethics: The views of informal carers. *International Journal of Geriatric Psychiatry*, 17(1): 35–40.

Suggested Reading

1. Fulford, K. W. M. 1989. *Moral Theory and Medical Practice.* Cambridge: Cambridge University Press.
2. Hughes, J. C. 2001. Views of the person with dementia. *J Med Ethics* 27: 86–91. [PMC free article] [PubMed].
3. Kitwood, T. 1997. *Dementia Reconsidered. The Person Comes First.* Buckingham: Open University Press, p. 91.
4. Parsons, K. 1997. The male experience of caregiving for a family member with Alzheimer's disease. *Qual Health Res* 7: 391–407.
5. Pinner, G. 2000. Truth-telling and the diagnosis of dementia. *Br J Psychiatry* 176: 514–5. [PubMed].
6. Pratt, C., V. Schmall, and S. Wright. 1987. Ethical concerns of family caregivers to dementia patients. *Gerontologist* 27: 632–8. [PubMed].

7. Sabat, S. R., and R. Harré 1994. The Alzheimer's disease sufferer as a semiotic subject. *Philosophy Psychiatry Psychology* 1: 145–60.
8. Schneider, J., J. Murray, S. Banerjee, and A. Mann. 1999. Eurocare: a cross-national study of co-resident spouse carers for people with Alzheimer's disease: I—factors associated with carer burden. *Int J Geriat Psychiatry* 14: 651–61. [PubMed].

Ethics Summary Table

How to Care for People with Dementia

Dignity and quality health care provider:
Assessment
Community resources (e.g., for respite care)
Confidentiality
Relations with family
Telling the patient the diagnosis
Professionalism
The health care provider needs to educate the family
The dignity of care
Quality of care
For Family:
Make decisions throughout the disease
Realize how much attention they need
The trauma of moving a person to a facility is on both sides – patient and family
The decision is about making sure the person receives the attention needed
To be aware of the types of care available
The importance of advance directives
End-of-life decisions
Lack of support
Need for information

Chapter 25

Surrogate Decision Makers

If a patient is unable to make decisions, someone else must provide direction in decision making as the surrogate decision maker. A surrogate decision maker is the advocate for incompetent patients.

Health Care Consent Act (HCCA)

Section 10 of the HCCA makes it clear that the health practitioner proposing the treatment must decide whether the patient is mentally capable of consenting to the particular treatment recommended. If the health practitioner wants to get a second opinion, it is open to him or her to do so, but this is not a requirement before treatment is administered to the person. The health practitioner is deemed to be the "expert" in determining capacity as defined by the HCCA in respect to treatment within his or her area of practice and expertise.

Circumstances where the legislation requires that a "capacity assessor does the assessment."

This "capacity assessor" in the legislation is the person acting as the assessor and is required to perform capacity assessments as defined by the "Guidelines for Conducting Assessments of Capacity" established by the Attorney General and dated June 7, 1996.

A person of advanced age or persons with physical or mental disabilities may still be capable of making all or some decisions for themselves. The definition of capacity does not make exceptions for age, physical disability or mental disability.

The key is whether the person understands the information that is relevant to making a decision and can appreciate the reasonably foreseeable consequences of the decision or lack of the decision.

The place where a person resides or is living temporarily does not determine whether they are capable or incapable in respect to some or all decisions they are making. The test of capacity applies to all situations wherever the person lives or is receiving treatment. Just because a person has consented to move to a long-term care facility and required a variety of care services and procedures, there is no automatic implied consent to the procedure.

Default Surrogate

The American Bar Association has been trying to define the surrogate in different states. The Default Surrogate Consent Statutes July 2017's explanation is given below. The descriptors in the chart are generalizations of the statutory language and not quotations, so the statutes must be consulted for precise meaning. The default surrogacy statute language varies from state to state, and the listed descriptors hold the following definitions:

- An adult includes any person who is 18 years of age or older and is either the parent of the patient, is married to the patient, is the adult child of the patient, or an adult sibling of the patient.
- Close friend (adult friend) is one who has maintained regular contact with the patient as to be familiar with the patient's activities, health, and religious or moral beliefs (https://www.americanbar.org).

  What is a health care surrogate designation? It is a document naming another person as your representative to make medical decisions for you if you are unable to make them yourself. You can include instructions about any treatment you want or do not want, similar to a living will.

Power of Attorney

A medical or health care power of attorney is a type of advance directive in which you name a person to make decisions for you when you are unable to do so. In some states, this instruction may also be called a durable power of attorney for health care or a health care proxy.[1]

A *health care proxy* (also referred to as a durable power of attorney for health care) is a document that appoints someone to make medical decisions for you if you are in a situation where you can't make them yourself. You must choose your proxy thoughtfully since he/she will be acting on your behalf.

If your doctor has already written a do-not-resuscitate (DNR) order at your request, your family may not override it. You may have named someone to speak for you, such as a health care agent. If so, this person or a legal guardian can agree to a DNR order for you.[2]

A *Durable Power of Attorney* for health care is a document that lets you name someone else to make decisions about your health care in case you are not able to make those decisions yourself. It gives that person (called your agent) instructions about the kinds of medical treatment you want.

Advance Directives

The definition of best in health care decision is when the best decision for the individual might not always be the best decision reached based on medical facts alone. The commitment to patient choices also led to a development framework to ensure patient preference when the patient is unable to make a decision, such as advance health care directives and leaving a will.

The following is the hierarchy of substitute decision makers (SDMs) in the Health Care Consent Act, s.21.[3]

1. Guardian of the person with authority for health decisions
2. An attorney for personal care with authority for health decisions
3. A representative appointed by the Consent and Capacity Board
4. Spouse or partner
5. Child or parent or person with the right of custody
6. Parent with the power of access
7. Brother or sister
8. Any other relative
9. Office of the Public Guardian and Trustee

Presumption of Capacity

The presumption of capacity means that a person is presumed to be mentally capable concerning treatment, admission to a care facility, and personal assistance services. This assumption is intended to give the benefit of the doubt to the patient or resident, to respect an individual's right to control his or her own life, and to honor that person's power over decisions that are being made concerning his or her person. What does it mean to be "mentally capable"?

"Capacity" under s. 4 of the HCCA[4] means that the person "can understand the information that is relevant to deciding on the treatment, admission, or personal assistance services, as the case may be, and can appreciate the reasonably foreseeable consequences of a decision or lack of decision."

One of the most common problems is when the requirement for disclosure, understanding, voluntariness, and competence creates conflict when considering research in subjects for which these conditions cannot be met. Such groups would include those with impaired cognition such as those with Alzheimer's or are critically ill and children and organizations that are particularly susceptible to overt coercion such as prisoners. Complete avoidance of research in these subjects is not practical as it would necessarily eliminate research in fields such as pediatrics, critical care, and trauma. Moreover, exclusion of these items in all analysis is inappropriate as these populations would unable to derive benefits from participation.

Surrogate Consent

The application of *surrogate consent* has been applied to particular populations who are unable to meet the requirements necessary to achieve individual informed consent. In this situation, a proxy or patient-designated surrogate is invited to provide substituted judgment based on the patient's known or perceived convictions. However, few discuss their wishes about participating in research in advance and among populations such as children, the prior discussion is not possible. To protect these people, many suggest the use of surrogate consent only when the proposed research poses minimal risk and the opportunity for a direct benefit to the subject.

Notes

1. Mayo Clinic Staff. 2014. Living wills and advance directives for medical decisions. *Mayo Clinic.* Accessed at URL: https://www.mayoclinic.org/healthy-lifestyle/consumer-health/in-depth/living-wills/art-20046303.
2. Hiraoka, E. et al. 2016. What is the true definition of a "Do-Not-Resuscitate" order? A Japanese perspective. *Int J Gen Med*, 9: 213–220.
3. ACE. 2013. Tip Sheet # 2 HIERARCHY of Substitute Decision Makers (SDMs) in the *Health Care Consent Act.* Accessed at URL: http://www.acelaw.ca/appimages/file/Tip%20Sheet%20TWO%20-%20Hierarchy%20of%20SDMs%20FINAL%20Sept%202013.pdf.
4. Wahl, J. 2008. 25 common misconceptions about the *Substitute Decisions Act and Health Care Consent Act.* ACE. Accessed at URL: http://www.acelaw.ca/appimages/file/25%20Common%20Misconceptions.pdf.

Suggested Reading

1. DeMartino, E.S. et al. 2017. Who decides when a patient can't? *The New England Journal of Medicine*, 376(15): 1478–1482.
2. Wynn, S. 2014. Decisions by surrogates: An overview of surrogate consent laws in the United States. *Bifocal*, 36(1). Accessed at URL: https://www.americanbar.org/publications/bifocal/vol_36/issue_1_october2014/default_surrogate_consent_statutes.html.

Ethics Summary Table

How to Approach Surrogate Decision Makers

Spouse

Partner

Children

Parents

Named decision maker

Ethics committee and judge to appoint one if does not have any.

Someone 18 years of age or older

Close friend (adult friend) is one who has maintained regular contact with the patient

Health care surrogate designation is person as your representative to make medical decisions

The advance directive in which you name a person to make decisions for you

Durable Power of Attorney – a document that lets you appoint someone else to make decisions

Presumption of capacity means that a person is presumed to be mentally capable.

Chapter 26

Transplant Ethics

Ethics Dilemma

Although the relationship of the transplant surgeon to the patient entails all the usual ethical considerations such as informed consent, the doctor–patient relationship, and the evolution of experimental work to the standard of practice, there are unique elements in the field of transplantation that create additional ethical dilemmas.

- Since the beginning, transplantation has been an ethical issue; people attempted to transplant organs hundreds of years ago.
- The modern era of transplantation dates to just over 50 years ago when, in 1954, the first successful kidney transplant was performed between identical twins.
- Since then, the success of the field has expanded to include the robust organs – heart, lung, liver, pancreas, etc. The selling and buying of organs has to be the most significant challenge to ethics.
- The number of patients awaiting transplant and available organs lead to some ethical issues.

Congress

- In 1972, Congress passed legislation supporting the care of the patient with a terminal disease, which required a transplant.
- This was initially limited to a small segment of U.S. population who were chronically ill due to kidney failure and were on hemodialysis.

Shifting Donor Ethics

- Every donor determination of brain death needs to be assessed by a different team not involved in the care of the patient.
- As the demand for donor organs has increased, the profile of the cadaveric donor has changed over time. Early donors were young individuals usually involved in vehicular motor accidents or the victims of trauma. Recently, the profile of the cadaveric donor has shifted to the older donor whose death is more likely secondary to cerebral vascular accident or of cardiac origin. This distinction is essential in the context of organ distribution as the outcome of organ transplantation from the older donor is less ideal than the result from the younger donor.

United Network of Organ Sharing (UNOS) System

- Because of the multiple problems that the United States face regarding organ transplants, the UNOS made guidelines.
- Donor family must be given adequate informed consent;
- Be aware of the potential risk and understand this risk;
- There is a system for the end stage of disease called the Mayo Model for End-Stage Liver Disease (MELD) system.
- For the distribution of organs, the petitioner is assigned points based on objective promises that taken together dictate their chance of dying without transplantation.
- The altruistic method is in place and continues to be the driving force in United States.

  Organ distribution would be to assign a place in line to the most gravely ill patients. This method of delivery underlies the use of the MELD system for liver distribution.

Supply Demands

- Supply and demand correlate economics with payment for transplantation. Organ availability is limited.
- One argument against the buying and selling of organs is that this practice will undermine the system that currently exists, which is based on altruism.
- The commercialization of the organ is not ethical and not taken into consideration.
- The change in demographics of the cadaveric donor population raised additional issues in organ allocation. As older donors are accepted for transplantation, it has been established that kidneys and livers fare less well than organs from younger donors.

Ethics Issues

Transplant Tourism

Transplant tourism was developed for organ selling. This brought about ethical issues related to paying donors for their body parts.

In certain countries, sometimes it's been oversight and therefore led many patients the United States to travel to other countries this country to receive an organ.

Remuneration

- The U.S. law doesn't allow the exchange of organ for remuneration.
- The proposals of donor rumination is still in discussion.
- Paying to eliminate the waiting list for organ transplantation will direct most of the transplants to high society and middle class and will eliminate the lower class.

A weak or disadvantaged individual has the right to determine whether he/she exchanges a kidney for money. Furthermore, it is argued that the paternalistic attitude that the poor should not profit from the sale of their organs does not attempt to find other solutions for the economic disparities which exist among different groups within societies.

Many U.S. physicians feel obligated to inform patients that a life-saving organ is more readily available in another country through the existing program of allocation.

The UNOS Ethics Committee has issued the following statement regarding transplant tourism:

> the Committee would be remiss in failing to observe that the practice of transplant tourism might not exist but for the growing disparity between the demand for and supply of organs. It is the solemn obligation of the transplant community, not only to publicly condemn the exploitative practices of transplant tourism but to endorse ethically defensible policies, which will ultimately render such exercise unnecessary.

Living Related

- Allocation of organ is difficult and complex and raised many ethical issues.
- Living related donors open different ethical issues.
- Using a living related donor is becoming more common in organ transplants.
- Usually, it is a relative donating to another relative.

- In Germany and France altruistic donors are not used readily.
- In Germany and France, donor recipients are required to prove a long-standing relationship with their donors.

    The increasing disparity between the waiting list for solid organs and the cadaveric organs available has once again made live donors an increasingly important source of solid organs in the United States. In 2002, the number of live donors for transplant exceeded the number of cadaveric transplants done.

    The U.S. UNOS guidelines dictates that the donor must be given adequate informed consent with clearly articulated potential risks and must understand these risks and that there is "donor benefit" in a donation. Presumably, this relates to psychological benefit regarding improved self-esteem for being of help to another person.

Prisoners

- Federal law prohibits the sale of organs in the United States. The U.S. prohibition of the sale of organs dates to 1984. The World Health Organization issued a similar ban in 1994. The lack of observance of these prohibitions in other countries has led to the widespread commercialization of organs in those countries.
- The Chinese transplant community has used the organs from executed prisoners as a source for transplantation; the government has stated that both the prisoners and their families have given consent to organ donation, but the issue of the use of organs without permission, the crimes for which execution is employed in China and the use of political prisoners for organ donation have all been raised as questions in the lay press.
- Recent events in China have opened the door for transplant tourism.
- The Chinese transplantation committee uses organs from executed prisoners as a source of transplantation.
- The government has stated that both the prisoner and their family have given consent to organ donation.
- But without consent it is a crime and is being over overseen by the government.

Donor Strict Evaluation

- A potential solution is a nonprofit entity or governmental agency to conduct evaluation of donor requirements.
- Psychological state.
- The motivation of the donor needs to be addressed – sometimes the reasons are financial and sometimes they can be pressure.

The care of the cadaveric donor and the determination of "brain" or "cardiac" death has been separated from the transplant community. Intensivists have taken over the management of these patients; this addresses an inherent conflict of interest for the transplant community. The transplant community's primary concern is to serve the patient awaiting transplantation; this conflicts with the optimal management of the patient with head trauma or requiring end-of-life care.

Another set of ethical issues underlying transplants relate to the benefit versus harm considered in the context of both recipient and donor. With cadaveric donors, "harm" is less of a consideration and there is more emphasis on the potential benefits to the recipient. When one considers organ distribution, the interest accrued to one recipient of a given organ may be compared to the potential benefit if the organ is instead distributed to a different recipient.

Suggested Reading

1. Brown, M. 2017. Saturday Bird Droppings: Where the Orioles Still Haven't Started Christmas Shopping. *SBNation*, December 23. Accessed at URL: https://www.cam-denchat.com/2017/12/23/16813436/orioles-trade-rumors-manny-machad.
2. Cameron, J. S. & Hoffenburg, R. 1999. The ethics of organ transplantation reconsidered: Paid organ donation and the use of executed prisoners as donors. *Kidney International*, 55(2): 724–732.
3. Danovitch, G. M. et al. 2013. Organ trafficking and transplant tourism: The role of global professional ethical standards—The 2008 Declaration of Istanbul. *Transplantation Journal*, 95(11): 1306–1312.
4. Huang, J. et al. 2012. A pilot programme of organ donation after cardiac death in China. *The Lancet*, 379(9818) 862–865.
5. Manne, B. 2017. No clear path for prepayment and make whole premiums in bankruptcy. *Commercial Law World*, 31(1): 36.
6. Truog, R. D. & Miller, F. G. 2008. The dead donor rule and organ transplantation. *The New England Journal of Meidicine*, 359: 674–675.
7. UNOS. 2010. Ethical principles in the allocation of human organs. *OPTN*. Accessed at URL: https://optn.transplant.hrsa.gov/resources/ethics/ethical-principles-in-the-allocation-of-human-organs/.
8. UNOS. 2017. UNOS Ethics Committee Meeting. Accessed at URL: https://unos.org/event/optnunos-ethics-committee-meeting-12/.

Ethics Summary Table

How to Approach Transplants Issues

Transplant raises many issues particularly on donation.
These issues are too many to be treated in a review chapter.
Physicians should be suspicious of any mistreatment and misinformation.
Donors should not be coerced.

Brain death needs to be assessed with set parameters.

UNOS system is the standard.

Remuneration for donation is not ethical.

A living related donor's donation should be freely given and not an action of force.

A long term relationship is needed to be approved a living related donation.

Prisoners as donors is not standard practice in the United States but is allowed in other countries.

Chapter 27

End-of-Life Ethics Issues

Ethical Dilemma

Health care professionals are faced with many challenging ethical dilemmas and controversies that are difficult to resolve in today's workforce. Among these issues is the controversial "right to die" debate. Patients have many reasons to die but first and foremost is when they lose hope and dignity. The patient's right to die will be examined from the perspective of a nurse who is a Cancer Center Coordinator. Ethical principles that must be considered are beneficence and autonomy.

As stated by Lalwani et al.,[1] the "principle of beneficence focuses on doing good for others and to take action for the best interest of the patient" and "the principle of autonomy explains that the patient has a right to make decisions for him/herself." Health care providers (HCP) are on the front lines of these situations since it is nurses who tend to the medical needs of dying patients on a daily basis. Another relevant term to define is palliative care.

The World Health Organization (WHO) describes palliative care (PC) as caring for a patient with no intent to either hasten or postpone death; furthermore, WHO emphasizes that PC views are dying as a normal process of life. Research has shown that cancer patients near the end of life are taught to use forms of palliative care often.

To further understand the magnitude of this type of ethical dilemma, it is helpful to define a few more terms. In an article by Keefe,[2] he sets these critical four terms as:

- *Life-sustaining treatment*: This, in the view of the person, provides healthcare for the person concerned and is necessary to sustain life.

- *Mental capacity*: The 2005 Act states that a person lacks ability if impairment or disturbance in their mind means they cannot make a specific decision at the time they are required to make it. There is a presumption that an individual has the capacity.
- *Euthanasia*: The active and intentional termination of a person's life...The key is that someone other than the individual has control and acts to end the individuals' life, with the intention to kill...
- *Assisted suicide*: Providing someone with the means to end their own life, facilitating or encouraging a person to commit or attempt to commit suicide. Assisted suicide may be physician-assisted or amateur-assisted suicide. It differs from euthanasia in that the individual retains control of the process.

There are currently five states in the United States that have legalized physician-assisted suicide laws (Table 27.1). This highlights the significance of HCP familiarizing themselves with the "right to die" concept.

Compassion & Choices

Compassion & Choices works to improve access to a full range of end-of-life options for terminally ill adults, including access to better pain management, palliative care, enrollment in hospice, and aid in dying. Compassion & Choices encourages people to document their wishes in an advance directive to ensure their end-of-life decisions are known.

The policies would be significantly improved by clearly distinguishing between "assisted suicide" and "active euthanasia," which are criminal acts, and the withholding, withdrawing and refusal of treatment and aid in dying. These clarifications will assist health care providers who practice in jurisdictions where aid in dying is legal to understand the distinction between aid in dying and assisted suicide.

Compassion fatigue has been defined as a combination of physical, emotional, and spiritual depletion associated with caring for patients in significant emotional pain and physical distress.

Described by cancer care providers, emergency room personnel, chaplains, and first responders, among others, compassion fatigue may impact HCPs in any specialty when, in the process of providing empathic support, they experience the pain of their patients and families.

HCPs and Dignity

Communicating with family during this process is of utmost importance. In a review of literature conducted by Materstvedt,[3] he found that two main reasons

Table 27.1 States with Right to Die

State	Date Passed	How Passed (Yes Vote)	Residency Required?	Minimum Age	# of Months until Expected Death	# of Requests to Physician
1. California	October 5, 2015	End of Life Option Act (ABX2-15)	Yes	18	Six or less	Two oral (at least 15 days apart) and one written
2. Montana	December 31, 2009	Montana Supreme Court in Baxter v. Montana (5-4)	Yes	–	–	–
3. Oregon	November 8, 1994	Ballot Measure 16 (51%)	Yes	18	Six or less	Two oral (at least 15 days apart) and one written
4. Vermont	May 20, 2013	Act 39 (Bill S.77 "End of Life Choices")	Yes	18	Six or less	Two oral (at least 15 days apart) and one written
5. Washington	November 4, 2008	Initiative 1000 (58%)	Yes	18	Six or less	Two oral (at least 15 days apart) and one written

patients request assisted dying include loss of dignity and loss of autonomy in their daily life functions at the end of life. A case-study review found nothing controversial in a cancer patient's right-to-die decision, since it offered a dignified death with relief from suffering. In the state of Oregon, where there are currently right-to-kill laws enacted, less than 3% of all deaths were those that were assisted to die. A study that was referenced in Nevidjon and Mayer,[4] "reinforces the need for continuing education in end-of-life care and showed the second highest rated core competency needed in communicating about death and dying. It was found that up to 60% percent of patients receiving the end-of-life care did not feel they were informed entirely of prognosis, the possibility of death or alternatives in communications with their health care providers…"

The Right to Die

When one begins to think about a patient's right to die, research revealed that there is a gap in the literature on how nurses handle and feel about this topic. This was interesting to find since, in many cases, the nurse is the one closest to the patient and family during these difficult times. In the instance of oncology nurses, it is crucial for each nurse to understand and learn to deal with feelings that arise during the disease process of cancer. As the study by Comasetto[5] pointed out, understanding how one perceives death assists with one's own emotions. Whether one views death as a part of life, as a sense of powerlessness, empathetically, or seeks to understand death through faith; the nurse must be prepared emotionally to face the end of the patient. This is an essential concept for HCP administrators that work in settings such as oncology. Ensuring that your staff is adequately prepared and trained for this eventuality is just as important as ensuring that their skill level is up to par. Evaluation and understanding of ethical principles are equally important when discussing a patient's right to die. As a HCP, a highly asked question is: Is it right to respect a patient's autonomy and let the patient die? The principle of freedom should assist in understanding that a patient's wish should be respected regardless of the positive or negative outcomes.

Considering that state laws govern the acts of euthanasia and assisted suicide, right-to-die decisions (since euthanasia and assisted death is illegal in most states) currently deal with instances such as refusing treatment or choosing palliative care as opposed to aggressive curative care. HCPs work toward the best interest of the patient; however, this is why this topic is so controversial. The critical terms of euthanasia are reported in Table 27.2.

Lalwani et al.[1] remind us that "Best interests of patients resides in alleviating suffering and preserving life." Take for instance a terminal cancer patient who is receiving palliative care but is not able to relieve suffering due to extreme pain. In this scenario, how can one preserve life, yet not alleviate suffering and still be keeping the patients best interest in mind? This illustrates the blurred line with

Table 27.2 Key Terms for Euthanasia

- Beneficence – Doing good for others and taking action in the best interests of the patient.
- Autonomy – Patient has a right to make decisions for him/herself.
- Palliative care (PC) – Caring for a patient with no intent to either hasten or postpone death.
- Life-sustaining treatment – Health care that is necessary to sustain life for a person.
- Mental capacity – The 2005 Act states that a person lacks capacity if an impairment or disturbance in their mind means they cannot make a specific decision at the time they are required to make it.
- Euthanasia – The active and intentional termination of a person's life.
- Assisted suicide – Providing someone with the means to end their own life, assisting or encouraging a person to commit or attempt to commit suicide.

regards to the right to die. Research has shown that many people would rather die by choice, instead of prolonged treatments or going through an undignified illness. Interestingly, a recurring theme in the majority of these articles was in support of individuals having the right to factual information from their health care provider on end-of-life choices and should be able to make the informed decision about their right to die.

Education for All

It is evident that a patient's right to die decision directly affects health care providers involved in their care. The majority of HCPs that care for patients with terminally ill conditions watch people suffer at the end of their lives. A recurring theme in this review of the literature was how nurses need to be educated on communication regarding end-of-life and right-to-die decisions. This brings up that education in cultural beliefs is just as important. Many times HCPs lack knowledge of their patient's cultural and religious beliefs that pertain to life-and-death situations. HCPs that provide care to the terminally ill must be able to differentiate a decision made by a patient made in fear or misconception of the prognosis as opposed to an explicit autonomous choice that they are prepared to die. The HCP needs to be able to assist the patient to weigh the risks and benefits associated with their decision while keeping in mind enhancing the quality of life and still being able to justify the actions of the HCP. This takes us back to a fundamental role of the HCP as a patient advocate. The fact that patients feel they were not given complete information during their end-of-life discussions highlights the importance of preparing HCPs to deal with these types of encounters.

To live or to die is not an easy decision and assisting with an HCP to provide loving care and support to the patient and the family is even more difficult. There are no tools that HCPs used during this process except their own experience and learning from others. Neither the school training nor most of the hospital wards are places for learning these essential tools.

We strongly suggested introducing this training into schools since the population is growing older and issues about death will be more familiar everywhere.

In the meantime, many hospitals have developed services to assist in this transition in which a physician, nurses, and social services work together to support the patient and their family during this process—service that could be critical in the training of HCPs.

By those experiences and training, we might be able to prepare a young HCP to have the capabilities to handle the choice of death or the actual death of a patient appropriately.

The stress of taking care of this patient can affect the HCP. The HCP can be influenced by these experiences (Table 27.3).

Autonomy

It is suggested by the research that there is an ethical justification for respecting the independence and being beneficent with regards to the end-of-life care for the HCP, "Seriously ill people need end-of-life options. It is a basic human right to live and die with one's dignity intact."

Regarding standard ethical theory, respecting dignity can also be aligned with having respect for people and their free choices. People are then enabled to make decisions about their treatment.

Among other things, this grounds the practice of informed consent that should be respected by the nurse.

Although much of the debate lies in the discussion of cases where people are unable to make choices about their treatment due to being incapacitated or having a mental illness that affects their judgment.

A suggested way to maintain autonomy is for the person to write an advance directive, outlining how they wish to be treated in the event of them not being able to make an informed choice, thus, avoiding unwarranted paternalism.

Table 27.3 Experiences by Health Care Provider

4 categories:
• Experiencing death as a natural cycle of life
• Experiencing impotence before the death of the other
• Experiencing death with the help of faith
• Experiencing empathy facing the possibility of death of the patient

Future implications include developing curricula in schools and at work for new communication strategies to better prepare for the end-of-life care.

The economic health crisis brings to light the fact that this same financial pressure may lead to the perspective that euthanasia is much less costly than palliative care. Therefore, better equipping HCPs with the tools necessary to assist with end-of-life care autonomously may help alleviate the burden that may soon be placed on them regarding the right to die.

As HCPs, it is important always to consider that each case is different, and our duty should be to help each provider make the best decision for the patient and ultimately give them their say in a quality of life that is bearable for them in their terminal state.

With the new services dedicated to this issue, the importance of faith, comfort, and experience of the team is providing the basis for the end-of-life support and treatment.

Aid in dying is an end-of-life care option in which mentally competent, terminally ill adults request their physician to provide a prescription for medication that the patients can, if they choose, self-administer to bring about a peaceful death.

Aid in dying is not assisted suicide. Suicide is an inaccurate term when used to describe the rational and well-thought-through decision to end one's life if mentally competent, terminally ill, and suffering.

The term suicide conjures up the image of someone who is depressed, distraught, or suffering from a mental illness or other condition that may be treatable, allowing that person to live out a full and hopefully productive life.

From previous publication: Guerra, A.L. and Frezza, E. E. 2017. To die or not to die: this is the dilemma! *Journal of Epidemiology and Public Health* 2(1): 150–3. ISSN 2471-8211; http://dx.doi. org/10.16966/2471-8211.138.

Notes

1. Lalwani, E. et al. 2015. Case report: Discontented life versus peaceful death. *International Journal of Nursing Education*, 7(2): 176–178.
2. Keefe F.J. et al. 2005. Partner-guided cancer pain management at the end of life: a preliminary study. *Journal of Pain Symptom Management*, 29(3): 263–272.
3. Materstvedt, L.J. (2013). Palliative care ethics: The problems of combining palliation with assisted dying. *Progress in Palliative Care*, 21(3): 158–164.
4. Nevidjon, B. & Mayer D. (2012). Death is not an option, how you die is: Reflections from a career in oncology nursing. *Nursing Economics*, 30(3): 148–152.
5. Comassetto, I. (2014) Being nurse at a chemotherapy center with the death of an oncologic patient. *Escola Anna Nery Revista De Enfermagem*, 18(3): 503–509.

Suggested Reading

1. A State-By-State Guide to Physician-Assisted Suicide-Euthanasia. 2015. Accessed from URL: http://euthanasia/procon.org.
2. Chan, W., K. Lam, W. Siu, and K. Yuen. 2016. Chemotherapy at end-of-life: an integration of oncology and palliative team. *Support Care Cancer* 24: 1421–7.
3. Havil, G. and Nichols, J. 2013. No conflict between nursing and helping a patient die with dignity. *Kai Tiaki Nursing New Zealand*, 18(11): 26–27.
4. Knowles, M. (2012). A right to die: an ethical dilemma. *Nursing & Residential Care*, 14(8): 430–432.
5. Moir, C., et al. 2015. Communicating with patients and their families about palliative and end-of life care: Comfort and educational needs of nurses. *International Journal of Palliative Nursing*, 21(3): 109–112.
6. Storch, J. 2015. Ethics in practice: At End of Life – Part 1: Challenges and opportunities for professional growth when providing end-of-life care. *Canadian Nurse*, 11(6): 20–21.

Ethics Summary Table

How to Approach End of Life

Death represents an ethical challenge for physicians.

The patient has the right to die with dignity.

Team approaches are now used to determine this situation and relieve pain in the end stage of the disease.

Team approaches and set protocol are used in this situation.

Presumption of patient to be capable of decision making.

If patient is suffering and terminal, this could be the best ethical decision.

Involve family and decision makers.

Surrogate decision.

Compassion and explanation of the choices.

States are different and have different legislation that needs to be followed.

Education about these issues is needed.

Autonomy of the decision respecting the person and their dignity.

Euthanasia is allowed only in a few states.

OUTSIDE AND INSIDE THE BOX

Chapter 28

Clinical Research and Institutional Review Board (IRB)

Ethics in Research

There is no greater area of ethical concern for government and the general public than clinical research demonstrating patient safety and autonomy. A potential proceeding benefit to society can be the direct result of the study but with careful regimentation.

Some international, national, and local regulation or regulatory bodies had been developed to help the standard by which clinical research is to be conducted. The growing presence of industries sponsoring clinical research creates new questions.

Ethics in research is evidenced by the creation of many guidelines and rules worldwide.

Ethics for the U.S. Food and Drug Administration (FDA) is essential in setting a high standard for safety when human subjects are involved.

The Council for the International Organizations of Medical Sciences (CISM) in collaboration with the World Health Organization issued guidelines that addressed the specific International Ethical Guidelines for Biomedical Research Involving Human Subjects to regulate the research studies that involve human subjects. The goal is to apply the Declaration of Helsinki.

Current ethical standards in clinical research stipulate that maintenance of patient autonomy and freedom from coercion is critical. Through the process of informed consent, full disclosure of all research procedures, risks, benefits, alternatives, and withdrawal opportunities should be delineated. This must be done on a level that is comprehensible to the subject, and this comprehension must be demonstrated. When informed consent is not possible, the use of surrogate consent is appropriate only when risks are minimal and a direct potential benefit exists. To maintain the trust of the public, it is critical that all research be conducted with the highest ethical standards and that the interest of individual research subjects is continuously analyzed and kept as the top priority.

Historical Steps

The Nuremberg Code. The most dramatic and well-known chapter in the history of research with human participants began on December 9, 1946, when an American military tribunal opened criminal proceedings against 23 leading German physicians and administrators for their willing participation in war crimes and crimes against humanity.[1]

As a direct result of the trial, the Nuremberg Code was established in 1948 stating that "The voluntary consent of the human participant is essential," making it clear that participants should give consent and that the benefits of research must outweigh the risks. Although it did not carry the force of law, the Nuremberg Code was the first international document that advocated voluntary participation and informed consent.[2]

The Declaration of Helsinki, developed by the World Medical Association, is a set of ethical principles for the medical community regarding human experimentation. It was initially adopted in June 1964 in Helsinki, Finland and has since been amended multiple times, lastly in 2000.

Research with humans should be based on the results from laboratory and animal experimentation; research protocols should be reviewed by an independent committee before initiation; informed consent from research participants is necessary; research should be conducted by medically/scientifically qualified individuals; and risks should not exceed the benefits.[1]

The Tuskegee Syphilis Study (1932–1972), also known as the Public Health Service Syphilis Study, was a clinical study conducted in the area around Tuskegee, Alabama. This study became notorious because individuals enrolled did not give informed consent and were not informed of their diagnosis.[3]

The Tuskegee Syphilis Study led to the Belmont Report and establishment of the *National Human Investigation Board* and the requirement for the creation of IRB.

The Belmont Report. The Belmont Report is a report created on April 18, 1979, by the former U.S. Department of Health, Education, and Welfare (which was renamed Health and Human Services). The report entitled "Ethical Principles and Guidelines for the Protection of Human Subjects of Research" is an essential historical document in the field of medical ethics. The Belmont Report explains the unifying ethical principles that form the basis for the National Commission's topic-specific reports and the regulations that incorporate its recommendations.[4]

Thalidomide. In the late 1950s, Thalidomide was approved as a sedative in Europe, but it was not accepted in the United States by the FDA. The drug was prescribed to control sleep and nausea throughout pregnancy, but it was soon found that taking this medicine during pregnancy caused severe deformities in the fetus.[1]

U.S. Senate hearings followed, and in 1962, the "Kefauver Amendments" to the Food, Drug, and Cosmetic Act were passed into law; drug manufacturers were required to prove to the FDA the effectiveness of their products before marketing them.

Clinical trials. Clinical trials in medicine are clinical studies, research protocols, or medical research studies. The most commonly performed clinical trials evaluate new drugs, medical devices, biologics, or other interventions on patients in strictly scientifically controlled settings and are required for regulatory authority (U.S. FDA) for approval of new therapies. The goals of these clinical trials are to establish survival rates and quality of life.[5]

IRB Issues

The Office of Human Research Protection was established in 1991 to oversee ethical aspects of human subject research and resulted in the formation of IRBs. Central to the charge of IRBs was to maintain the principles put forth in the Belmont Report. *Respect for persons* requires that research subjects be treated as autonomous individuals capable of deliberation about personal goals. Moreover, this principle states that vulnerable subjects are entitled to protection from exploitation. *Beneficence* is defined in the Belmont Report as an obligation to minimize potential harm and to maximize potential benefits.

The Belmont Report continues to be an essential reference for IRBs that review proposals involving human subjects to ensure that the research meets the ethical foundations of the regulations.

Many IRBs have developed standard language and a standard format to be used in portions of all consent documents. The standard language is typically designed for those elements that deal with confidentiality, compensation, answers to questions, and the voluntary nature of participation. If a non-English speaking subject is unexpectedly encountered, investigators will not have a written translation of the consent document and must rely on oral translation. Investigators should carefully consider the ethical/legal ramifications of enrolling subjects when a language barrier exists. If the subject does not understand the information presented, the subject will not be informed and consent may not be legally valid.[6]

The obligation of beneficence applies to both individual investigators and society. Thus, risks and benefits specific to the research subject must also be considered against the risks and benefits that effect the general community as a result of experimentation. Lastly, the principle of *justice* states that no specific group is unfairly utilized merely because of their natural availability, manipulability, or compromised situation. Moreover, when research results in the development of therapeutic interventions or devices, justice demands that the benefits not only be available to those who can afford them.

The Importance of Informed Consent

Central to the informed consent process is the provision of information to the research subject. In therapeutic trials, the potential benefit of the therapeutic intervention above that of standard care must be articulated as well as the perceived or postulated risks.

The second and perhaps most important piece of the informed consent process is the subject's comprehension of the material provided. Documents outlining the specifics of the intervention and the research plan should be submitted, reviewed thoroughly with each topic and all questions should be answered in detail. The right of each patient to withdraw at any time should be stated.

- Respect, justice, and informed consent is a crucial step for medical permission.
- The second most important part of the informed consent process is the subject's comprehension of the material provided.
- The patient has to decide with autonomy in a respectful way.
- Often the patient chooses a therapy even when evidence suggests a superior alternative, and many patients also refuse therapy once a stand-alone treatment exists in all trials. Comparing different therapies and close patient monitoring must be maintained.
- Some surgery, some placebos, or some medication can be controversial.
- For instance, in some countries you can give a saline injection as a pain medication, in the United States you cannot. Yet despite this some patients feel better just after the water injection.
- This shows that the response is much more mental than physical.

If investigators enroll subjects without an IRB approved written translation, a "short form," or consent document, in a language the subject understands should be used to document. The required signatures on a short form are stated in 21 CFR 50.27(b).[7]

Animals in Research

A physician involved in biomedical research is often faced with the dilemma of determining whether the use of animals in such research is ethical. For example, is it ethical to use animals in research for the benefit of humanity and the benefit of other animals? Most of the biomedical research is conducted using animals with highly developed nervous systems and the ability to perceive pain and distress.

Various regulations and guidelines are in place to promote quality animal care, to ensure that research manipulations are performed with the least possible number of animals, and to minimize the potential pain and distress these animals may experience. Specifically, two federal laws (the Animal Welfare Act promulgated by the U.S. Department of Agriculture and the Health Research Extension Act enacted by the Public Health Service) apply. Guidelines are found mainly in the Public Health Service Policy on Humane Care and Use of Laboratory Animals. The Institute of Laboratory Animal Resources' Guide for the Care and Use of Laboratory Animals (referred to as "the Guide"), and the Federation of Animal Science Societies' Guide for the Care and Use of Agricultural Animals in Agricultural Research and Teaching are the other areas where legislation is present.

The American Medical Association (AMA) recognizes and supports the need for responsible animal use in biomedical research in the following statement:

> Researchers should include in their protocols a commitment to ethical principles that promote high standards of care and humane treatment of all animals used in research. Further, they should provide animal review committees with sufficient information so that useful review can occur. For their part, institutions should strengthen their animal review committees to ensure adequate review of all research protocols involving animals. The appropriate and humane use of animals in biomedical research should not be unduly restricted.[8] Local and national efforts to inform the public about the importance of the use of animals in research should be supported the development of suitable alternatives to the use of animals in research should be encouraged among investigators and supported by government and private organizations. The selection of other options ultimately must reside with the research investigator.

Notes

1. University of Missouri-Kansas City. History of Research Ethics. Accessed at URL: http://ors.umkc.edu/research-compliance-(iacuc-ibc-irb-rsc)/institutional-review-board-(irb)/history-of-research-ethics.
2. University of Nevada, Las Vegas. History of Research Ethics: Accessed at URL: https://www.unlv.edu/research/ORI-HSR/history-ethics.
3. Mandal, J. et al. 2011. Ethics in human research. *Trop Parasitol*, 1(1): 2–3.
4. Wikisource. 2015. Belmont Report . Accessed at URL: https://en.wikisource.org/wiki/Belmont_Report.
5. Science Daily. Clinical Trial. Accessed at URL: https://www.sciencedaily.com/terms/clinical_trial.htm.
6. Russell-Einhorn, M. 2017. Non-English speaking research subjects: What's in the regs? SchulmanIRB. Accessed at URL: http://www.sairb.com/non-english-speaking-research-subjects-whats-regs/.

7. US FDA. 2018. A Guide to Informed Consent: Information Sheet. Accessed at URL: https://www.fda.gov/RegulatoryInformation/Guidances/ucm126431.htm.8. AALAS. Use of Animals in Precollege Education. Accessed at URL: https://www.aalas.org/about-aalas/position-papers/use-of-animals-in-precollege-education.

8. AALAS. Use of Animals in Precollege Education. Accessed at URL: https://www.aalas.org/about-aalas/position-papers/use-of-animals-in-precollege-education.

Suggested Reading

1. Council for the International Organization of Medical Sciences (CIOMS). 1993. *International Medical Guidelines for the Biomedical Research Involving Human Subjects.* Geneva, Switzerland: CIOMS.

2. Internati, C. 2006. Clinical research. In: E.E. Frezza (Ed.) *Professionalism and Ethics in Surgical Practice.* Woodbury, CT: Cine-Med.

3. Kampmeier, R. H. 1972. The Tuskegee study of untreated syphilis. *South Med J* 65: 1247–51.

4. Kampmeier R. H. 1974. Final report on the "Tuskegee syphilis study." *South Med J* 67: 1349–53.

5. Murray, T. H. Meeting Ethical Challenges: From Tuskegee to Stem Cells. *Course Hero.* Accessed at URL: https://www.coursehero.com/file/159214/Tuskagee-notes/.

6. Resnik, D. 2018. Research ethics timeline. *National Institute of Environmental Science.* Accessed at URL: https://www.niehs.nih.gov/research/resources/bioethics/timeline/index.cfm.

7. Sims, J.M. 2010. A brief review of the Belmont Report. *Dimens Crit Care Nurs.* doi: 10.1097/DCC.0b013e3181de9ec5.

8. United States National Commission for the Protection of Human Subject of Biomedical and Research Behavioral Research. 1979. *The Belmont Report: Ethical Principal and Guidelines for the Protection of Human Subjects of Research.* Washington, DC: DHEW Publicaiton.

9. World Medical Association. 1964/ 2000. Declaration of Helsinki, as amended by the WMA 52nd General Assembly, Edinburgh, Scotland, October 2000.

Ethics Summary Table

How to Look at Research and Trial

Advancement in medicine came from research.

Research needs to be regulated.

Regulation is necessary for humans and animals.

After World War II, the need for set research protocol was required.

Research finalized to people's benefit.

Clinical trials in advance is the type of study where patients need the most information.

The IRB is the office that in each hospital overview and protect patients' rights in trials.

Language and standard should develop nationally.

Informed consent needs to inform the patient of all the pros and cons and the drop out clause.

Patient autonomy needs to be respected.

Documentation should be available.

Any addition to the project needs to have a new approval.

Animal research has protocols and rules that need to be applied.

Chapter 29

Ethics Role with Manufactories

Relationships Between Pharma and Health care

Relationships between health care professionals and pharmaceutical companies have become ethical issues due to the potential threat to the safety of patient care and public trust of health care professionals. These relationships become a conflict of interest when the pharmaceutical companies supply gifts to the physicians and other health care professionals to influence pharmacological treatment decisions. These decisions are made by personal attention and not by professional values. The physician was always considered the "soft target" of the industry since they can access the prescribers and possess a powerful influence on their decisions, making them susceptible to conflicts of interest. There are different laws that govern relationships between the pharmaceutical industry and health care professionals.

One is in Vermont called Vermont's Prescribed Product Gift Ban and Disclosure; the other is the Physician Payments Sunshine Act.

On the other side of the coin is Advanced Medical Technology Association AKA AdvaMed. The primary goal of AdvaMed recognized there were inconsistencies in the manner that business was being conducted and made changes.

Health care providers are vulnerable to a conflict of interest with the power pharmaceutical companies carry in influencing the prescriber. The survey asked about awareness and perceptions of Vermont's law requirements regulating the relationship between pharmaceutical companies and health care providers.

Ethical Issues

Ethical issues regarding the gift-giving of pharmaceutical industry representatives to health care professionals including nurses have been raised. Two of the laws and regulations that govern this activity are the Physician Payments Sunshine Act (PPSA) and Vermont's Prescribed Product Gift Ban and Disclosure Law. PPSA is a 2010 U.S. health care law enacted to increase transparency of financial relationships between health care providers and pharmaceutical manufacturers by mandating disclosure of the connections. Under this Act, pharmaceutical manufacturers are required to report all payments and gifts made to physicians. This Act was passed to decrease the physicians' influence on prescribing medication and to increase the safety, quality of patient care, and to recover and strengthen trust in the health profession by the public. Under PPSA, nurse practitioners (NPs), physician assistants (PAs), nurses, and other allied health care providers are excluded from this.

Vermont's Prescribed Product Gift Ban and Disclosure Law also passed for the same reason. This law sternly requires all pharmaceutical companies to report all payments, meals, medical samples and gifts made to health care providers. However, health care providers are not required to report any gifts from pharmaceutical companies. Some pharmaceutical companies go as far as sponsoring meetings, lectures, and conferences. It is estimated that about $57 billion is spent yearly on marketing by the pharmaceutical industry just in the United States. This is twice the amount that is spent on research and development. Physicians have a great deal of influence in making decisions on patient treatment, including prescription medications and recommending over the counter medications. Taking this into consideration, physicians are now being targeted by pharmaceutical companies to encourage and influence prescribers by supplying them with gifts, permanently placing patient care in a compromising position. This sets them in a vulnerable state because decisions are being based on "personal interests rather than professional values."

Furthermore, in the recent years, patients have attained more power in their care by acquiring knowledge of medications and treatments, giving them more autonomy in the control of their care. They are also becoming more aware of the influence pharmaceutical companies have on prescribers. Trust in their health care provider is another issue that may be raised if treatment decisions are not made impartially. There is also a global organization AdvaMed that represents "business interests in all markets." This includes the Food and Drug Administration (FDA) and Centers for Medicare and Medicaid Services (CMS). Their mission is "to advocate a legal, regulatory, and economic climate that advances global health care by assuring patients can have access to benefits of medical technology." AdvaMed noted discrepancies with how business was being conducted and developed a code of ethics which took effect on January 1, 2004. Smaller companies were having difficulty competing with larger pharmaceutical companies in the gifts that were being provided. The rationale for the code of ethics was to "level the playing field for the health care industry" and make sure business is being conducted appropriately and fairly. Under this code of ethics, gifts are still allowed but only for educational purposes or the benefit of the patient, and it must be under $100. No cash or equivalent may be gifted.

Financial Relationship

As ethical issues are raised concerning the economic relationship between pharmaceutical company representatives and prescribers, laws are being put into action to increase transparency by requiring pharmaceutical companies to report any and all gifts. These requirements are, in essence, increasingly putting registered nurses (RNs) in a vulnerable position, because they are now being targeted by the pharmaceutical industry who know they have the power to influence the prescriber in the making a decision about treatment.

These decisions become unethical when personal interests are placed on the importance of the patient, and the beneficence of the patient is not taken into consideration. Unfortunately, PPSA does not provide a systematic way to investigate for compliance or erroneous information submitted even though federal enforcement is very observant. On a positive note, since the adoption of AdvaMed's Code of Ethics, the way business is conducted has changed. Now pharmaceutical companies, large or small, can no longer offer incentives but focus on quality, education, and support, improving the overall method of business. Conflicts of interest should be placed ahead of personal interests.

Industry Changes

However, with the emergence of the AdvaMed rules, everything has changed. AdvaMed has members worldwide in the health care industry. Their mission is "to advocate a legal, regulatory and economic climate that advances global health care by assuring patients can have access to the benefits of medical technology." AdvaMed represents business on a global level. They represent business interests in all markets including here in the United States with the FDA and CMS.

In 2003, AdvaMed released its Code of Ethics which changed the way the health care industry did business. This Code of Ethics took effect on January 1, 2004.

The purpose of this is to level the playing field for the health care industry. As stated in the preamble of the Code of Ethics, the industry must respect the obligation of health care professionals to make independent decisions regarding medical products.

The purpose of the Code of Ethics was to allow for the ability of the smaller companies do business without having to compete with the larger companies for "gifts."

For example, it is entirely acceptable for the industry to pay for a physician to travel to an educational conference but it is not acceptable for the industry to pay for a day at the spa or a round of golf. Subsequently, expenses paid can only be for the person attending the conference and not for spouses, children, or friends. The rules even go so far as to state that the conference or educational activity must be in a "facility conducive to the effective transmission of knowledge."

However, AdvaMed is not the only organization with members in the health care industry. PhRMA (Pharmaceutical Research and Manufacturers of America) also have a code of ethics that is applied to those in the pharmaceutical industry. Their voluntary system of relationships took effect on July 1, 2002. The rules are quite similar to the Code of Ethics by AdvaMed.

By having to justify your expenditures, the industry has had to cut down on the number of amenities they give away. And those facilities have to be for educational purposes. This has increased the number of educational programs available to health care professionals. It does not matter if the educational program is geared strictly to the use of a product or provides education that improves our practice. The ultimate goal is to be able to continually improve our profession and the care that is given the patient.

Health care professionals must continuously be on the lookout for educational programs where the fee may be minimal or even free. This encourages attendance which is a benefit to both the health care worker and industry.

Since the adoption of the AdvaMed Code of Ethics, the strategy of doing business has changed. Salespeople can no longer attract business simply by offering incentives for their customers. The industry has had to focus more closely on quality products and keep a closer eye on their competition. They strive to provide something their competition cannot, which is quality, education, and support.

Big companies know the rules and enforce them quite fiercely, and health care professionals who try to work around the Code of Ethics very often find that this is an impossibility. Many companies have adopted a zero-tolerance policy, and since this also coincides with the Anti-Kickback law from the federal government, the fines for non-compliance can be as high as $10,000–$50,000 and imprisonment.

There is no doubt that the AdvaMed Code of Ethics has changed the way the business of health care is run. We have dealt with those with lesser moral values than our own.

Suggested Reading

1. Adams, J. 2011. Nurse prescribing ethics and medical marketing. *Nursing Standard* 25(29): 62–6.

2. Chimonas, S. & Rothman, D.J. 2005. New federal guidelines for physician–pharmaceutical industry relations: The politics of policy formation. *Health Affairs*, 24(4). Accessed at URL: https://www.healthaffairs.org/doi/abs/10.1377/hlthaff.24.4.949.

3. Frezza, E. E., 2008. Relationships with manufacturing companies: What are the rules? In L. Randall(ed.) *Professionalism & Ethics in Surgical Practice*. Woodbury, CT: Ciné-Med, Inc. pp. 339–42.

4. Gorlach, I. and G. Pham-Kanter. 2013 Brightening up: the effect of the physician payment sunshine act on existing regulation of pharmaceutical marketing. *Journal of Law, Medicin & Ethics* 41(1): 315–22.

5. Grande, D. 2010. Limiting the influence of pharmaceutical industry gifts on physicians: Self-regulation or government intervention? *J Gen Intern Med*, 25(1): 79–83.

6. Grundy, Q. 2012. The physician payments sunshine act and the unaddressed role of nurses: an interest group analysis. *Policy & Nursing Practice* 13(3): 154–61. doi:10.1177/1527154412465196.

7. Grundy, Q. 2014. "My love-hate relationship": ethical issues associated with nurses' interactions with industry. *Nursing Ethics* 21(5): 554–64. doi:10.77/096973301351 11360.

8. Jones, J. W. Esq., Medical Device Manufacturer Relationships, Physician's News Digest, March 2005.

9. Kennedy, A. G., C. J. Possidente, and R. G. Pinckey. 2013. Awareness and perceptions of Vermont's prescribed product gift ban and disclosure law by prescribers and pharmacists. *Journal of Pharmacy Practice* 26(1): 36–42. doi:10.177/089719001245193.

10. Sullivan, T. 2018. Compliance challenges within medical affairs. *PoliyMed*. Accessed at URL: https://www.policymed.com/2014/06/compliance-challenges-within-medical-affairs.html.

Ethics Summary Table

How to Look at Manufactories Role

The role of manufacturers has a potential threat to the safety of the patient.

The push of medicine had enjoyed no rules for a while.

Physicians had experienced the benefits of trips and other perks for a while.

There was the fear among pharmaceutical companies of physicians being biased in their choices.

Now gifts are banned.

Now patients request meds after watching ads on TV.

Paying travel expenses for education is still acceptable.

Companies are now watched over and are fined if they are found to be at fault.

Physicians must be balanced and impartial in their choice of treatment.

The benefit to the patient is, first and foremost, the most important concern.

Chapter 30

Ethics in the Event of Bioterrorism

Terrorism

Terrorism, per the Department of Defense, is the "unlawful use of violence, often motivated by religious, political or other ideological beliefs, to instill fear and coerce governments … in pursuit of goals that are usually political." While another agency's definition might be a slightly different variation, terrorism includes the use of violence, creating fear, involving coercion, and is unlawful. Bioterrorism is the deliberate use of bacteria, viruses, and toxins as weapons intended to create social disruption via mass panic, hysteria, and fear causing illness and death.

September 11, 2001, was the day the world as we knew it changed. Terrorism, although a known occurrence, had never hit so close to home. That day will forever be etched in the minds of many Americans. That day, the United States was under attack. It became apparent that as health care professionals we needed to be prepared, not if it happened again but when it happened again. And, it did. A week later, on September 18, anthrax-laced letters were mailed to several media offices and two U.S. Senators. These events killed five people and infected seventeen others. It was evident that the use of biological agents was an easy method to disseminate disease among the population and that, as a nation, we needed to be prepared. National Security was heightened, and funds were directed to help fund bioterrorism preparedness plans. Nurses need to be ready, break away from their traditional role, and recognize and respond when these events occurred again.

Federal Programs

Several federal programs have been initiated to assist communities in enhancing their preparedness for events involving biological or chemical weapons of mass destruction. Community preparedness is far from perfect. Local health care, emergency care, EMS, law enforcement, and the FBI have been trying to implement responses for possible disaster planning and to improve real-time local patient health care capacity to enhance the response.

Development of standard education and training curriculum on terrorism and biological agents into health care training programs and expansion of federal and state programs to assist communities in developing increased public awareness and educational programs have increased, particularly after the September 11 attacks.[1]

We previously reported the problems with health care and the need for adequate plans and policies to apply to health care, which includes the Emergency Medical System (EMS) response to the full treatment and decontamination in emergency rooms and hospitals.

Several federal programs have been initiated to assist communities in enhancing their preparedness for events involving biological and other agents of mass destruction, such as the Metropolitan Medical Response System (MMRS) program. Community preparedness is far from perfect. It is a significant challenge to prepare for an unknown event without a clear-cut indication of whom to protect and from whom protection is needed.[1]

The Cost of Security

The task force of the Council on Foreign Relations reported that the United States remains dangerously unprepared to prevent and respond to a catastrophic attack on U.S. soil.

Security is not free. Health care incurs costs when it invests in measures to protect the portion of infrastructure that it owns or controls. Dollars spent on security could contribute to the further erosion of programs designed to support the local people who need the most care, and some hospitals do not have deep enough pockets to change and add security systems.

Most of the time, we think about chemical warfare agents as a military issue.

Several recent events have demonstrated that civilians might be exposed to these agents as well. The resources of U.S. communities to respond to chemical incidents have been designed primarily for industrial agents, but must be expanded and developed regarding incident management, agent detection, protection of emergency personnel, and clinical care.[2]

Hospital-Based Planning for Chemical and Biological Terrorism

The weapons of mass destruction (WMD) are a threat, and all health care facilities must prepare for this risk. Every health care facility is a vital part of the community response system and must be ready to respond. A terrorist attack using WMD can occur in any location, urban or rural. The fundamental precept in hospital-based planning for bioterrorism events includes having a comprehensive emergency room disaster plan. The Joint Commission for Accreditation of Healthcare Organization (JCAHO) environmental health care standards and approach to disaster planning and management form the basis for a stable bioterrorism response plan. Preparation, education, and training are imperative. Clinicians must maintain a high index of suspicion for the use of bioterrorism agents, be able to make a rapid diagnosis, and initiate experimental treatment. However, the person should be familiar with the plan and know when to activate it. A recognized incident command system should be used. Hospital leadership must be aware of facility capabilities, capacity and should also have plans for expansion of service to meet the surge in demand. The command center should coordinate the emergency personnel teams. If the method is implemented, stress management and psychological support will play an essential role in recovery.

Health care facilities are an essential component of an emergency response system but, at present, are poorly prepared for an incident.

The most significant challenge may be the sudden presentation of a large number of contaminated individuals. Gathering information on contaminated patients has been based on the traditional collection of material from those with military experience, which is not directly applicable to the civilian. Essential elements of the health care facility response plan include prompt recognition of the incident, staff and facility protection, patient decontamination and triage, and medical therapy and coordination with the external emergency response and public health agencies.

Controversial aspects include the optimal choice of personal protective equipment, the establishment of patient decontamination procedures, the role of chemical and biological agent detectors, and potential environmental packs and water treatment systems.

Fung distributed 174 questionnaires among graduate students in Hong Kong. 164 (94%) were answered and returned. Almost all the nurses (97.6%) considered the hospital authority (government health department) as the agency more involved in emergency response. 97% found themselves inadequately prepared to respond to disasters. And even though 84.8% believed that there was a protocol that existed at their hospital for dealing with disastrous events, only 61% had read the procedures. When asked about what action they would take if disaster struck at work, 38.4% would follow hospital protocol, 34.8% would wait for instructions, 34.4% would alert people before escaping, 15.2% would evacuate patients, and 7.3% would leave as soon as possible.

Professionalism during Stressful Situations

It is human behavior that during stressful situations we become overwhelmed and do not react appropriately, but we need to evaluate ourselves and the problem and think about the community and how to defend our community. As a physician, we must continue to support our profession most ethically. We must apply our knowledge both in the hospital and in a camp in a rural area. At all costs, we must avoid confrontation or discussion with other physicians because this will not allow us to do our job and will not portray the picture of professionalism to patients and other personnel. Therefore, during this uncertain time, we need to be sure to adhere to the following principles:

- Help patients, people, and staff.
- Remember our ethical oath.
- Do not confront other professionals or physicians because this is not the time and will not give an excellent example of professionalism to other people around you.
- Make sure to have an organized shift that will avoid tiredness.
- Follow the directive of the command center.

Education

Are we educated to deal with a disaster? Out of physicians and nurses, 6.2% rated their education as not prepared at all, 20.6% rated their training as not very ready, 62.4% rated their training as somewhat prepared, and only 6.2% rated their training as very prepared. Questions related to the nurse's knowledge regarding biological agents, such as anthrax, smallpox, botulism, and tularemia, was also assessed using true–false questions. 55.7% gave correct responses when asked about signs and symptoms of anthrax and flu-like illnesses. Smallpox was estimated with questions concerning vaccination. While 29.4% responded that they would recommend smallpox vaccination to their family, 49.0% would not. Also questioned was the nurse's perceived likelihood of a biological, chemical, or nuclear attack. Although most nurses (>50%) believed that a biological or chemical attack was somewhat likely, 39.7% thought that a nuclear attack was somewhat likely and 38.1% thought it was not very likely. It was clear that schools needed to be part of the community's response efforts and the perception that an event was unlikely to occur are necessary to be addressed.

With the reality of such potential future threats, there has been an increased awareness of public health nurses being at the forefront.

We must, therefore, receive adequate training to assure competency when dealing with these infectious agents that may otherwise go undetected being that they are odorless, colorless, and tasteless. The first step is identifying who needs to know how to do what and the ability to fulfill that role.

It is essential that we receive the necessary education to remain competitive in the subject matter and be able to act, if necessary, during a bioterrorist attack. It is critical for nurses to become familiar and have some essential core competencies when responding to emergencies that can be used when the community's health is at risk. Education should be on-going and not a onetime training opportunity.

Core competencies identified the chain of command, resources available, existing threats, and the signs and symptoms of the potential agents and how to treat them.

Notes

1. Frezza, E.E. 2005. The challenge of the hospitals and health care systems in preparation for biological and chemical terrorism attack. *Journal of Social Sciences*, 1(1): 19–24.
2. Frezza, E. E. 2004. The challenge to hospitals and health care systems preparing for WMD. *ACMQ Focus*, 14(1): 11–12.

Suggested Reading

1. Aghaei, N. and M. Nesami. 2013. Bioterrorism education effect on knowledge and attitudes of nurses. *J Emergencies, Trauma, and Shock* 6(2): 78–82.
2. American Nurses Association. 2010. Who Will be There? Ethics, the Law and A Nurse's Duty to Respond to a Disaster. Accessed at URL: https://asprtracie.hhs.gov/technical-resources/resource/1207/who-will-be-there-ethics-the-law-and-a-nurses-duty-to-respond-in-a-disaster
3. Bradley R. N. 2000. Health care facility preparation for weapons of mass destruction. *Prehosp Emerg Care* 4(3): 261–9.
4. Brennan R. J., J. F. Waeckerle, T. W. Sharp, and S. R. Lillibridge. 1999. Chemical warfare agents: emergency medical and emergency public health issues. *Ann Emerg Med* 34(2): 191–204.
5. Council on Foreign Relations Task Force Report: Emergency Responders: Drastically Underfunded. 2003. *Dangerously Unprepared, Report of an Independent Task Force.* New York: Council on Foreign Relations.
6. Evers S. and L. Puzniak. 2005. Health service applications. Bioterrorism knowledge and emergency preparedness among school nurses. *J School Health* 75(6): 232–37.
7. Flowers L. K., J. L. Mothershead, and T. H. Blackwell. 2002. Bioterrorism preparedness. II: the community and emergency medical services systems. *Emerg Med Clin North Am* 20(2): 457–76.
8. Frezza E. E. and M. Chiriva-Internati. 2005. The quality of homeland security and healthcare systems: The Texas rangers initiative. *J Social Sci* 1(3): 194–6.
9. Fung, O. W. M., A. Y. Loke, and C. Lai. 2008. Disaster preparedness among Hong Kong nurses. *JAN Original Res* 62(6): 698–703.

10. Gebbie, K. and K. Quereshi. 2002. Emergency preparedness and disaster preparedness: core competencies for nurses. *Am J Nursing* 102(1): 46–51.
11. Hadstad, D. and K. Kearney. 2000. Emergency: bioterrorism. *Am J Nursing* 100: 33–5.
12. Macintyre A. G., G. W. Christopher, E. Eitzen Jr, R. Gum, S. Weir, C. DeAtley, K. Tonat, and J. A. Barbera. 2000. Weapons of mass destruction events with contaminated casualties: effective planning for healthcare facilities. *JAMA* 283(2): 242–9.
13. Manning, M. and F. Henretig. 2002. Bioterrorism. *JSPN* 7(2): 49–53.
14. McFee R. B., 2002. Preparing for an era of weapons of mass destruction (WMD). Are we there yet? Why we should all be concerned. Part 1. *Vet Hum Toxicol* 44(4): 193–9.
15. Mondy, C., D. Cardenas, and, M. Avila. 2003. The role of the advanced practice nurse in bioterrorism preparedness. *Public Health Nursing* 20(6): 422–31.
16. Rebmann, T. 2005. Health care preparedness. *Occupational Health and Saf* 74: 11.
17. Schultz C. H., J. L. Mothershead, and M. Field. 2002. Bioterrorism preparedness. I: the emergency department and hospital. *Emerg Med Clin North Am* 20(2): 437–55.
18. United States Department of Defense. Accessed from URL: www.defense.gov.
19. Wikipedia. 2018. Florence Nightingale. Retrieved April 22, 2016. Accessed from URL: http://en.wikipedia.org.

Ethics Summary Table

How to Implement WMD Responses

A system needs to be in place in the event of a WMD attack regarding the following:

Policies
Plans
Ambulance traffic
Personal protective equipment
Training personnel
Personnel requirements
Education
Treatment
Surveillance system
Decontamination system

Chapter 31

Ethics Conflicts in Rural Health

The Unbalance

According to the U.S. Census Bureau, any community whose total population is under 50,000 is considered a rural area. Recent estimates indicate that nearly 25% of the total U.S. population now resides in rural areas.

Practice in a rural environment may introduce additional difficulties in abiding by the standards stated by the American Medical Association's (AMA's) principle of medical ethics.

While more than 25% of the U.S. population live in rural areas, it is estimated that only 10% of physicians practice in a rural setting. Lack of access to care is apparently not a solely rural issue, however; as a profession and society we need to wrestle with the ethical question of not providing access to care to all our citizens. As a matter of ethics, this impacts both organized medicine as well as the broader points of access to health care in our country.

The most challenging task is to provide adequate health care in rural communities and how to maintain ethical standards of practice as a rural health provider.

Stressors in Rural Areas

Residents who live in these communities depend on health care workers to meet their medical needs in a timely and accessible manner. Since there is a significant lack of primary care providers working in rural areas, it is a constant battle for physicians and nurses to achieve success in the delivery of quality health care. Therefore, health care professionals must be prepared to multitask and possess the confidence to manage a multitude of patients living in rural communities independently.

Apparently, there is little dispute regarding the stressors that create ethical problems for health care providers throughout their careers. When discussing the ethics of health care, the majority of attention has been focused on those who provide care in high acuity areas such as in hospital emergency rooms and intensive care departments. Rural health physicians must face unique geographical, cultural, and socioeconomic challenges that can complicate the delivery of health care to patients and are unlike those of their city counterparts who work in more developed, urban areas. The most common themes that result in ethical conflicts experienced by rural health providers include working with limited resources, lack of professional support, and complex dual professional–patient relationships. Consequently, a physicians in rural settings must be supported in their quest to identify sources of ethical conflict and ways to manage these problems in practice.

Physician Specific Issues

A physician in a rural setting is vulnerable to the complexity of the environment in which he or she lives; a close-knit community, limited resources, lack of support and coverage, and limited access to specialty services. These characteristics of a rural community can produce ethical situations that a non-rural physician may not have to face.

The physician can find themselves in situations where being a health care provider overlaps with friendships created within the community. In cases where client relationships last for a prolonged period, providing objectivity during health encounters is impaired. This can lead to the unacceptable disclosure of personal information and a violation of the ethical standards of practice. When they interact with patients in social settings, privacy and anonymity are disrupted. This can result in good situations which cause role strain for nurses related to the inability to remain nonjudgmental. Personal relationships with patients can create an additional barrier to the delivery of health care when physicians struggle to keep their own life private and protect the confidentiality of their patients. Practicing open communication will be helpful because it articulates the need to set boundaries with patients. Limiting the exchange of personal information is in the best interest of rural health providers because it will help maintain a therapeutic patient relationship while avoiding the risk of unethical encounters.

Telemedicine

Another challenge represented when living in a "state" of isolation from other health care providers is how to communicate and find help when necessary. Telemedicine has been applied to help hospitals without specialists, countries without doctors. Critical care, burn, pulmonary, etc. consults have been used around the country thanks to telemedicine in an area where there is a lack of providers or coverage. A rural physician living and working in a smaller community usually loses the anonymity that an urban surgeon might enjoy. The local grocery store, the local restaurant, or even local churches are all places where they will undoubtedly encounter their patients. The very nature of rural practice raises questions such as, how does a country physician find anonymity and how is a patient's confidentiality protected.

A rural physician or a nurse practitioner, in most cases, is in practice alone. He or she may be on called upon 24 hours a day, seven days a week. A rural physician needs to prepare a great deal to plan for an extended leave of absence.

Frequently, locum tenens must be hired for coverage, often at the surgeon's own expense. More often than not, continuing medical education (CME) is sacrificed for patient care, which is apparently a problem in practice.

Telemedicine is often used within the same system in health care to provide real-time medicine off campus. In a similar fashion, groups of critical care doctors are giving consultations 24 hours a day to a hospital in New York or Florida by telemedicine. Therefore, we think that telemedicine can also be used to help any physician in a rural area to decrease their isolation and bring support and different competencies to the table. That can be done by a physician to another physician or nurse. We envy telemedicine as physicians can communicate and share their experiences in different rural areas, since they might have similar cases, and have the diverse experience of consulting in a rural area to a major medical center as well.

The AMA's principle of ethics mentions the maintenance of the patients' rights and confidentiality. Although the physician may do everything possible to maintain that secrecy, smaller communities have a high percentage of neighbors treating neighbors. An equally typical scenario is for the physician to be questioned by the neighbors and friends of a patient at a community event about the status and recovery of a patient. A friend asking about a neighbor may not realize the delicate position a community practitioner is placed in and the ensuing ethical dilemma that must be addressed.

Health Care Providers' Issues

Most information obtained from the review of the literature indicates that three common themes surround ethical issues most often faced by working in rural communities. The first moral issue involves the unequal distribution of resources in rural areas. It is these same patients that often require a higher level of care due to poorly managed health conditions. Also, the shortage of health care providers who practice in a rural community places patients at a disadvantage since many will not readily have access to specialists who can provide care for their complex health needs. Health care providers must struggle to provide care to patients who would benefit significantly from being referred to a more qualified practitioner but are unable to receive additional care due to financial difficulty or travel barriers. For many patients, it may be intimidating to travel to a larger city to obtain health care. For others, such as the poor or elderly, transportation to a larger hospital or care facility may present an obstacle too daunting to overcome. The ethical challenge then becomes providing the best possible care to patients even with a limited amount of resources. Financial and time constraints often limit the ability for continuing education because the institution they work for cannot afford to pay for educational opportunities. In fact, it is often unrealistic to allow the physician to take time off work for educational conferences when they may be the only health care provider for the community. It is essential that rural health care providers be given the opportunity to advance their education and improve their professional competency. Recognizing occupational limits and remaining within the skill of the practice will help avoid situations that cause ethical conflicts for a rural area.

A second issue is professional isolation. Historically, there has been a shortage of health care providers living and practicing in rural settings. Within the health care workforce, providers are taught the principle of professional collaboration. The rural physician is expected to exercise independently since other health care professionals may either be limited or unavailable. This lack of professional support can lead health care providers to make the unethical decision to provide care beyond their scope of practice. Furthermore, a physician who practices alone often feels obligated to continue to care for patients even when they are tired or overworked. When this occurs, the physician is more likely to risk burnout and endanger the health and safety of their patients.

Challenges

Rural physicians present both rewards and challenges to providers who choose to pursue a career in these communities. Physicians sometimes feel burdened by the constraints of scarce resources, lack of privacy, and professional isolation. If not managed effectively, these challenges can create ethical conflicts for nurses. The first recommendation is take an example from some medical schools which already institute rural curricula.

The second recommendation will be to build a telemedicine web system which will connect different physicians in rural areas with each other and will provide a more extensive health system of practitioners with the same daily issues.

Chapter from the Article: Frezza, E. E. and Beltran. C. C. 2017. Ethical nursing conflicts in rural health. *J Epidemiol Public Health Rev* 2(1): 1–3. http://dx.doi.org/10.16966/2471- 8211.137

Suggested Reading

1. Davis, R. and L. Weiss Roberts 2009. Ethics conflicts in rural communities: patient–provider relationships. In W. A. Nelson (ed.) *Handbook for Rural Health Care Ethics: A Practical Guide for Professionals*. Lebanon, NH: University Press of New England.
2. Doty, B. S., Heneghan, M. Gold, J. Bordley, P. Dietz, S. Finlayson, and R. Zuckerman. 2006. Is a broadly based surgical residency program more likely to place graduates in rural practice?. *World J Surgery* 30(12): 2089–93. Discussion 2094.
3. Finlayson, S. R., J. D. Birkmeyer, A. N. Tosteson, and R. F. Nease Jr. 1999. Patient preferences for location of care: implications for regionalization. *Med Care* 37(2): 204–9.
4. Lyckholm, L. J., M. H. Hackney, and T. J. Smith. 2001. Ethics of rural health care. *Crit Rev in Oncol/Hematology* 40: 131–8.
5. Mehrotra A., A. B. Jena, A. B. Busch, J. Souza, L. Uscher Pines, and B. E. Landon. 2016. Utilization of telemedicine among rural Medicare beneficiaries. *JAMA* 315(18): 2015–16.
6. New York medical society conference, New York, NY, 2015.
7. Thompson, M. J., D. C. Lynge, E. H. Larson, P. Tachawachira, and L. G. Hart. 2005. Characterizing the general surgery workforce in rural America. *Arch Surgery* 140(1): 74–9.
8. Tung, T. and C. H. Organ Jr. 2000. Ethics in surgery: a historical perspective. *Arch Surgery* 135(1): 10–13.
9. US Census Bureau. 2015. Urban and Rural Classification. Accessed at URL: http://www.census.gov/geo/reference/urban-rural.html.
10. Williamson, H. A., L. G. Hart, M. J. Pirani, and R. A. Rosenblatt. 1994. Market shares for rural inpatient surgical services: where does the buck stop? *J Rural Health* 10(2): 70–9.

Ethics Summary Table

How to Approach Rural Health

Lack of physicians and isolation can create problems.

Knowing most of your patients can cause conflicts.

Managing a disease outside of a physician's training is at times problematic.

Physicians struggle with their own private life and relationships.

Limited resources are available.

Telemedicine could help solve some of these problems.

Physicians have to deal with the constraints of limited resources.

Physicians can suffer from professional isolation.

There is a lack of medication in rural areas.

Index

Note: Page numbers in bold indicate tables.